AuthorHouse™
1663 Liberty Drive
Bloomington, IN 47403
www.authorhouse.com
Phone: 1 (833) 262-8899

Because of the dynamic nature of the Internet, any web addresses or links contained in this book may have changed
since publication and may no longer be valid. The views expressed in this work are solely those of the author and do not
necessarily reflect the views of the publisher, and the publisher hereby disclaims any responsibility for them.

Any people depicted in stock imagery provided by Getty Images are models,
and such images are being used for illustrative purposes only.
Certain stock imagery © Getty Images.

This book is printed on acid-free paper.

ISBN: 978-1-7283-5795-9 (sc)
978-1-7283-5796-6 (e)

Library of Congress Control Number: 2020906534

Print information available on the last page.

Published by AuthorHouse 09/21/2020

author HOUSE®

HOW TO
DOMINATE ANY
MARKET

◆◆◆◆◆◆◆◆◆◆◆◆◆◆◆◆◆

Turbocharging Your Digital Marketing and Sales Results

by Lonnie D. Ayers, PMP, BSC, SAFe

CONTENTS

HOW TO
DOMINATE ANY
MARKET

◆◆◆◆◆◆◆◆◆◆◆◆◆◆◆◆◆◆

Turbocharging Your Digital Marketing and Sales Results

LONNIE AYERS

7256 Keith Donaldson Rd

Freetown

IN

47235

812 3405581

Lonniea39@yahoo.com

CHAPTER ONE

MY STORY

In 2008, I found myself once again working in the Middle East, only this time, home based in Dubai, a place I had last worked in toward the end of 2001. I arrived just before the global financial crisis hit. Hired by SAP MENA[1] as a Senior Program Manager to rescue a failing SAP[2] Airline MRO[3] implementation, I was almost immediately asked to change hats and become an Industry Principal[4]. I was also asked to keep working as the SAP Program Manager on the entire Airline Implementation Project. This meant I was designated as the Go-To SAP guy and inserted into the now highly charged Steering Committee[5]. This was a quota carrying sales role which meant I was on the road 5 days a week.

---

[1] MENA means Middle East and North Africa

[2] SAP, the name of a German Software company, which roughly translated, means Software, Applications and Programs.

[3] MRO means Maintenance, Repair and Overhaul.

[4] Industry Principal, in this context, meant I ran a business with a full P&L.

[5] Steering Committees are typically composed of Senior Executives of a company, and have decision making authority for major Program and Project issues which arise.

Though the world economy went into a tailspin in September of 2008, and most of the SAP global sales pipeline disappeared overnight, in the Middle East, I was able to build a full sales pipeline and also run several SAP projects. Some of these projects were implementation projects while others were sales projects involving a cast of, well, a lot of people from a lot of different backgrounds and partners.

In short, I was a busy SAP Consultant[6] putting way too many miles on my body. My wife of 25 years was still living in Madrid, Spain without plans of joining me in Dubai. I was commuting back and forth to see her at least once a month and it was a solid 8 hour non-stop flight each way. We had never lived apart in 25 years of marriage, but I had always had traveling jobs, so at first, this wasn't too bad, but by the second year of this grind, I was deeply unhappy with the way things were. The money was fantastic, more than I had ever made in my life but as they say, 'money isn't everything'.

On one of my monthly trips home, I was moving something downstairs and managed to trip and fall from the first floor to the ground floor of my 3 story home. An MRI would reveal the now constant lower back pain was from a dislocated vertebra. Due to the economic crisis, us SAP Consultants were now in economy class on every flight. We were already mostly in economy class, but now, even the frequent long overseas flights were economy. That's how I found myself in the middle seat between 2 other guys at least as big as me on a 15 hour and 15 minute non-stop flight from Dubai to Atlanta.

Toward the end of my third year in this role, my boss, the Managing Director of SAP Middle East or SAP MENA, happened to be in Madrid at the same time I was passing through and asked to meet me for lunch. This never ends well. They had been pressuring me to take a permanent role (read pay cut) and I was looking

---

6. SAP Consultants are business consultants who design, configure and deliver SAP Software solutions.

for the exits. So at lunch that momentous day, with my back screaming at me, when he asked me point blank if he could count on me, I gave him my resignation.

My contract, as most Middle Eastern labor contracts do, required me to give them a 90 day notice while they only had to give me 30. Due to my very senior level position in the company, and unique knowledge of both SAP and the Defense Forces of the Middle East, they kept asking me to extend my departure date. They also kept trying to talk me out of departing at all, which, though flattering, just irritated me. Finally, in February of 2011, I left the company for what I thought would be the final time. To celebrate, my wife and I went to Tahiti for our 30th wedding anniversary, business class all the way, only to get struck by the Japanese Tsunami, and though we had a good time and all was fine in the end, we thought we were done for. That's a story for another day…

She Keeps Saying No

As the Senior Industry Principal responsible for the Aerospace & Defense, Travel & Transportation, Postal, Utility, Professional Services and Logistics industries throughout the Middle East, I had to submit an annual business plan. An Industry Principal runs a virtual business within the larger SAP organization, and 'owns' all aspects of the business, including: Sales and Marketing, Professional Services, Development, Consulting, Value Engineering, Business Transformation Consulting, Training and Support. In short, he has access to tremendous resources because the revenue expectations are extremely high.

Each year, after I submitted the marketing plan portion of my business plan, the director of marketing, a lady from Greece, would always tell me 'no' and follow it up with a recommendation to do more Inbound

Marketing. However, she couldn't really explain what Inbound Marketing was. Then one day, she invited me to a demonstration of Hubspot Inbound Marketing software. It was interesting, but I didn't pay too much attention to it. I just wanted to know how it could help me generate more leads so I didn't have to travel and network so much on my own.

We Incorporated from the UAE and Japan

It was during this time frame that my brother and I, who is also an SAP BW consultant, as well as international consultant and embedded systems engineer, had decided we needed to try to build a business so we could do more than just sell our own hours. Why? After all, as SAP consultants, the jobs were finding us. It was not and is not unusual to receive close to 100 calls and emails every day looking for our consulting services.

We Needed to Solve One Key Problem

The problem with consulting, as all consultants come to realize, is that you only have so many hours available to sell, and there is always an Indian who can do it cheaper, as long as it is off-shored. We did not and do not consider our skillsets commodities. Why not? Because as long as there is any risk to what you're doing, what you're doing isn't a commodity[7]. By definition, every project we did had some degree of risk involved. If it didn't, why is risk management a part of every project? Therefore, what we needed to do was develop a model where we could charge for the value we delivered but as well, attract and create more people just like us.

---

[7]   Implementing Value Pricing, Ronald J. Baker, Pg. 272

SAP Professional Services Provided the Business Model

As an Industry Principal, my special expertise was that I got to, at some level, know the entire SAP solution, end-to-end. In particular, it fell to me to determine what software packages would need to be licensed by a client to fully support their business processes. The process for doing this is somewhat complicated.

First, you will usually have an RFP[8] (Request for Proposal) that is typically organized by required features and functions rather than by business process. Then you will have to have created what is called a Solution Map, which maps the SAP Solution to the Business Processes. It takes a great deal of specialized industry knowledge as well as SAP knowledge to do this. You get this specialized knowledge from a combination of actual industry experience, Industry Principal training and certification provided by SAP and hands on implementation experience. The SAP Industry Principal is the person who has this knowledge, training, experience and business acumen.

Even he will typically have to consult with other experts to make a final determination of what software license packages are needed. Then this has to be priced out using a highly complex pricing tool. This information is then incorporated into an overall implementation plan, including consulting, training, hardware and support. SAP has over 1,300 products on their price list, so this can take some time. If you don't define all the required licenses, and you sign off on an RFP that says all requirements can be met, a client can and will demand 'free' software. Mistakes here can cost millions in lost revenue and lead to severe revenue recognition issues. This process of defining requirements and then determining the software required would prove very helpful in designing our business.

---

8. An RFP or Request For Proposal is a document used by a company to solicit offers from vendors. They can be as simple as a single page Purchase Order or as complex as many thousands of pages. I've worked on all types.

When you provide any kind of consulting service, such as SAP consulting, you need certain systems, like time sheets, expense sheets, payroll, sales and marketing. Due to my role, I had seen how the likes of SAP, Accenture, KPMG, IBM and many others had slowly but surely developed systems based on SAP that made the administrative nightmare of billing by the hour go away to be replaced by automation. SAP, however, is far too expensive and frankly speaking, complicated, for a start-up, so I used it as reference model and knitted together a Business Operating System (BOS) from various cloud-based systems, such as Quickbooks Online, Springahead, and Hubspot, and quite a few others.

My goal was to build an infinitely scalable business IT solution that worked whether I had only myself billable or 10,000 consultants billable. To a large extent, I succeeded. The BOS system I designed has been implemented by several of our customers, some of which have gone public with it or been bought out. In one case we know of, one of our customers was acquired, and the acquiring company chose to keep the BOS system in place rather than their own as it worked much more efficiently.

How Do We Generate Leads?

Once I had pulled the cord on the SAP job, I had to figure out how to generate leads, lots of them, and fast. I had already seen clearly that trade shows were far beyond our budget and didn't really generate leads. In fact, at one of the last trade shows I worked, we spent $50,000 and generated only 9 leads. You do the math on our cost per lead on that one. Our existing network was doing great – at generating jobs for us, but we wanted our own direct customers.

That's when I remembered my marketing director's advice to 'do more Inbound Marketing'. I was not a trained marketer at the time. Oh sure, I had an MBA and had been a presenter at innumerable SAP events on a large variety of subjects. I had built a global network of both SAP consultants and customers, which is what mostly drove the jobs my way. I had, in fact, been responsible for the marketing plan for SAP in the Middle East and as it turns out, i2 Technologies in Spain, many times. If anything, it was my 'domain expertise' that had worked in the past to help me generate almost one billion USD in total software and consulting revenue for these companies.

We needed a way to generate leads on a constant basis at a very low cost. We signed up for Hubspot, and as I do with every new skillset, I started working my way through all of their training, and building out our website, which was to become our digital lead generation machine. We did some things right while we missed the mark on other aspects our approach. At the time, there were no Hubspot partners, as the concept had not yet been launched and I was living in Spain, where there were even fewer marketing companies that I might have contracted, even if I had the budget, which I did not.

What We Missed

If I was starting over today, I would first concentrate on productizing my service offering (at least some part of it). That would have been a very difficult task to do in 2011, as what I did was and is very complex. I, like all SAP Consultants, benefitted from the systems and procedures that SAP had already developed.

For example, I am a Certified SAP Project Manager. I hold both the PMP[9] designation as well as holding the SAP ASAP[10] certification (SAP's project management methodology, now being rebranded as SAP Activate). I am also a Certified SCRUM Master and am SAFe (Scaled Agile Framework – Enterprise) Certified. It isn't a service offering that you can 'sell' online. It is a system that all successful SAP implementations use. I have even written some of the content you find within it (in the content delivered with your SAP Solution Manager) based on 'learnings' of mine from various projects. I also am an SAP Certified Materials Management (SAP MM) consultant as well as several other SAP modules. They all require you to deliver your implementation service onsite in most situations.

You should know that when we signed up for Hubspot, it was only a marketing platform and did not provide a CRM or Customer Relationship Management system. This was a major problem because you were supposed to keep track of opportunities inside the marketing system and that just didn't scale. We spent over 2 years evaluating CRMs, such as Salesforce CRM, SAP and Microsoft Dynamics and none of them really seemed to fit the bill. We were one of the first to sign up for Hubspot's CRM and it made all the difference. We should have started with a CRM, any CRM and worked backwards to the marketing system.

But of all the gotcha's, not having a content plan was our single biggest error. There were lots of reasons for this but the solution, which did not exist when we started our Hubspot journey, was the lack of a simple template that provided a visual way to create a content plan. It was a real a'ha moment when they came out with the content planning template. By then, we had produced the majority of our content and funnels, but without a real blueprint. We've since remapped and refined our own content into highly optimized funnels, all trackable within the Hubspot campaigns tool, which also didn't exist when we signed up for Hubspot.

---

9.   PMP, Project Management Professional, issued by the Project Management Institute or PMI.
10. ASAP, in this case, stands for Accelerated SAP

Finally, and this was huge for a service provider, we took too much time to realize that we were in the recruitment business. We were generating nice consulting opportunities all along, but without consultants, we would have to pass on them. That's why we pivoted and started aggressively getting people to submit their resumes so we could staff the projects. Seems like a no-brainer now, but at the time, it made it seem like our sales process wasn't working when, in fact, it was our delivery process that was not working. We've seen this same issue with clients who sell products and services across a wide range of industries.

What We Got Right

The whole Inbound Marketing approach can be boiled down to some fairly simple mechanical steps coupled with a methodology. You create a piece of content, say an eBook, and put it behind a form. You write a blog and put a Call-to-Action (CTA) in the blog to drive traffic to where the form is with your piece of content behind the form. A visitor completes the form, gets the promised content and you got yourself a lead, of some sort. You use email to pull people through your funnel until finally they are ready to buy, at which point they are passed to sales.

Being Senior Business Consultants, we didn't have any 'marketing content' when we started but we could create a lot of content, if we put our minds to it. Our Hubspot on-boarding consultant advised us to create checklists, white-papers and eBooks from existing documentation we had. So we started dreaming up such classics as **"The 10 step checklist for the SAP ASAP Project Preparation Phase"**, which is for the first phase of your SAP implementation, as an example. Over the years, we developed and published almost 400 downloadable pieces of content, 17 online calculators, and several online product selectors. A best seller has been the SAP Mindmap, which has been downloaded thousands of times and can be found printed out in SAP offices all of the world. Why was it such a best seller? Because it simplified a very complex subject.

We did all this using Hubspot. We've collected over 10,000 contacts, had over 400,000 SAP customers visit our site and we became a Hubspot reference customer. We also were invited to become Hubspot partners, which we did in 2015 and are now Gold Level partners. As a result, we have pivoted to now helping other SAP Partners, Customers and many other types of businesses with their marketing and sales, while still delivering SAP consulting services.

Keep in mind, when we signed up for Hubspot, they were only a five-year-old company and their software, though easy to use, didn't have anywhere near the capability it has today. So, when we started brainstorming on the content we would produce, they didn't have a campaign tool. To be honest, their on-boarding consultant didn't have a lot actual business experience, but was able to guide us through the process until we had our first offers up. We've gotten extremely efficient at producing all the components of an Inbound Offer over time. We've even had the opportunity to benchmark our 'production rate' against non-Hubspot marketing agencies. What we can do in less than an hour, they take days to weeks to do, and they miss a lot of steps.

What Our Customers Have Taught Us

As we began to acquire Hubspot customers, we also began to expand our service offering. What we found was that in order to fully leverage Hubspot, you also needed to master other forms of digital marketing, such as Google Pay Per Click (PPC) or Facebook ads. For our customers in the e-commerce space, learning how to use Amazon became a necessity. For some of our really large customers, we had to don our Supply Chain

Management hat and help figure out inventory management and related finance issues – which means we were doing the type of work we did as SAP consultants, again. That's what this book is about. The problems we see over and over again, the solutions to those problems and how you should implement them, or even if you should.

I hope you enjoy it. Now let's get started.

Who is this Book For?

This book is written for entrepreneurs. That covers a lot of ground, but the problems, solutions and principles I've laid out in this book apply whether you're just starting out or you have a multi-billion dollar multi-national business. How can that be, you might ask? Haven't we all been told to niche down, focus on just one narrow slice of the market?

It's because those big guys all started as small guys, often, just a one man show. However, having worked with and advised Fortune 500 businesses as well as helping to 'launch from zero' businesses, I've found they all have the same nine core sets of challenges, and each of those has a common set of solutions.

The major difference between setting up a successful business today and doing it 50 years ago is the simplicity. Fifty years ago, to set up an accounting system, was neither easy nor cheap. Today, a system like Quickbooks allows you to get it done in the morning. Forty years ago, setting up an international shoe manufacturing[11] supply chain was a Herculean effort. Today, you can do it online. Ease of doing things, though, has led to an explosion of suppliers, across all product and service categories.

[11.]   From working with the owner, Heyday Footwear

That's why today, the differentiating factor is Marketing and Sales - in that order. That's why I've focused this book on solving those issues. Sales is the lifeblood while marketing is the pump. Every business is now a digital business. Digital marketing now must be tightly integrated with every aspect of your business. Marketing and Sales have to have the systems in place so that they work together, not at cross-purposes.

How's this Book Organized

I've designed this book using a simple format: Problem->Solution->System. When you read through a problem, ask yourself if you are facing the same problem. If not, great, skip to the next chapter. If, however, you see yourself in the problem, then find the solution and the system. However, the greatest benefit will accrue to those who read through each chapter. Most problems are interrelated and most solutions require solving more than one problem. Just about all the systems are needed to resolve the problems and they all work together.

Now let's dive in.

CHAPTER TWO

PROBLEMS

Running a business today presents many complex challenges, unlike any faced in the past. But it is possible to compete and win, as long as you have the right business strategy[12] in place. You'll also need to have the right tools and tactics. In this book, I am going to lay out the common problems we've seen our customers face within their businesses. These are the problems we have encountered across a whole range of customers. Then I am going to provide a business blueprint you can follow to dominate any market.

What do I mean by a whole range of customers? I've helped existing SAP Partners fill their pipeline and close exceptionally complex deals. I've used the exact same strategies and tactics to help launch a coffee business, one of the most commoditized businesses on the planet. I've also worked to expand an existing insurance business to become one of the largest in their state, using a combination of Inbound Marketing and Paid Advertising - in 6 months.

---

[12]. Kaplan-Norton Balanced Scorecard, "A strategy is an integrated set of choices that position a firm, in an industry, to earn superior returns over the long run".

Many of my customers have been start-ups, some of which have already been bought out or went IPO (Initial Public Offering). While the methods I've learned have been used by many small and medium sized enterprises, some of the largest, such as the United Nations, have also become users of the systems I'll talk about in this book.

All of these businesses, regardless of industry sector, type of business or size of business, have had problems that fall into one of the nine 'problem buckets' I am about to explain. They've all benefitted, as could you, from the strategies, tactics, tools, and methodology, I will be explaining. You'll see the problems are actually very basic, foundational business issues as are the required solutions.

The Growth and Revenue Problem.

Achieving growth and increasing revenue is a major problem for most companies. Simply put, you are either growing or you are dying.[13] Those that hold steady or who are just standing still, treading water; they are just not going to make it. Why should that be? It really comes down to rising cost and competition. We'll go into both of these a little later on.

What do we really mean when we say a "Growth" or a "Revenue" problem? Well, this goes to the heart of everything else that a business is doing. What are the things that we always see when we ask a company "what's your annual revenue target"? Once they get to the point where you know they trust you, what you really find is that very few know the answer to this key question. Most just want to make as much as possible. If they

---

[13.]   Kaplan and Norton, "The Execution Premium: Linking Strategy to Operations For Competitive Advantage", 2008

are a giant company and they have an established business strategy such as the Balanced Score Card, then they will have an answer for this key question in the form of a 'Quantified Vision'.

But for the smaller guys, the short answer is "they just want to survive". You should know that it's really hard to budget when all you are really doing is "trying to survive".

Life Boat Stories

We've gotten a lot of what I call "Life Boat Stories". What's a life boat story? I've had customers come to me and tell me "listen, I have heard all about you but I'm three weeks from death as a company. What can you do to help me?" My answer: "Well to be honest with you I can help you dig your own grave".

That's sometimes what it gets down to. But I am willing to give it a shot.

I've had other companies come to me and say "Look, everything is going good, we don't really need any help". But then when you get into the numbers you find out they used to make 4 or 5 million USD a month but last month, somehow or another, they only made 20 thousand USD.

That generally is an oil rig platform on fire collapsing into the Gulf of Mexico[14] kind of situation.

This is when it's time to pull out all the stops and do something about it.

There're many other kinds of scenarios but they all kind of fall into what I call needing a "Life Boat".

What they are really asking me to do, most of the time is, they always want to see what I have done in the past, both for my customers and most importantly, for myself. Because, you know, I think we've got a pretty successful business going on, and what I tell them is what I want to help you do is, "build a speed boat, not just a life boat".

Image Courtesy of Creative Commons[15]

My Super Speed Boat Called "Lonnie's Life Boat"

I want to throw you a life raft or life line; I want to help you to build a speed boat and I want you to drive it yourself. I will initially do the work for you, but the truth is, you have to get your own speed boat so you can achieve those revenue growth goals that you have set.

---

15. https://en.wikipedia.org/wiki/Formula_4S_Powerboat_World_Championship

But more importantly, we've got to work with you to set realistic revenue and growth goals. We see the companies struggle to actually set a realistic revenue or growth target. Simply put, it means "commitment". It means that you know if I set this target now, I have to start thinking about realistic budgets. What's it going to take to get there. If what I did in the past hasn't worked, do I have enough wherewithal to invest more to get there in the future or do I put a stake through its heart. Quite frankly, sometimes, that's your only option.

A little later on, I am going to show you exactly how you can set a realistic growth target and what it will take to get you there.

Blood in the Water From Competition

There's one other issue that every business is facing – competition. It's never been easier or cheaper to start a business. That means every business is facing an ever-increasing number of hungry competitors. Hubspot's CEO Brian Halligan has estimated that there are now about 5 times the number of suppliers for each and every type of product and service as there were in 2011. For many companies with a growth or revenue problem, competition is bleeding them dry. In the digital marketing space, the ability of competitors to target your website visitors through a variety of tactics means you need a strategy to fight and win. It also means your offer has to be competitive. If it is not, marketing won't rescue your business and your life boat will sink like a lead balloon.

Summary

Most companies do not have established revenue goals or growth goals. Many come to us when it is too late to help them. We know how to do an honest assessment of your business situation and help you set realistic, achievable revenue and growth goals[16].

Do You Have a Not Sure What You are Selling Problem

I know that is sort of a weird name and a funny place to start a book, but this is a surprisingly common issue that we run across. Now, a lot of our customers are small, but some of our customers are fairly large, up in the $50 million dollar range and sometimes, way bigger than that. But nevertheless, what we have seen to be very common, across the board, is that when you ask them "what is it that you actually do or sell?" a surprising number of them really haven't thought that through.

---

[16]   Napoleon Hill, "Think and Grow Rich", The Ralston Society, 1937

What Do You Sell and How Do You Sell It

So the first problem that they are really faced with or what they are really asking for help with is to explain to us or help us define exactly what it is that we sell. This is particularly the case when it comes to services. Services is man-hours, if you get right down to it. Sometimes, there is a product. Sometimes there isn't a product. But there are always 'services'. They face the problem of how do you price that, how to get the word out, how to compete with the competition, especially the competition which is coming in from overseas.

What Channel Are You Selling In

They are faced with deciding what channel to sell it on; are they selling it face-to-face, are they selling online, is it a combination of traffic that's online that drives traffic off-line, are they able to sell it over social media, or do all the channels have to work together in order for them to answer the question: "what is it that you sell"?

Now, in our opinion, and in our experience, it's fairly straight forward to answer what it is that you sell if you have an established record. But if you are a startup, maybe you are pursuing the path of well "I am just going to do a minimum viable product (MVP)[17]".

Combination

What are you really selling there? A product? Or an Idea, a process, procedure? How much are you going to price it at?

This is a major problem for most companies. But there is an actual straight forward way that we will talk about a little bit later on as to how to really define that, so it facilitates you finding a selling solution and a marketing solution to help you solve this problem. So again, we are here to help you answer the question, "what is it that you sell?" So that it is no longer a problem, it is a known entity

---

[17.] Eric Ries, 2013, The Lean Startup: How Today's Entrepreneurs Use Continuous Innovation to Create Radically Successful Businesses

Do You Have a Marketing Performance Problem?

In previous chapters, we talked about a company's revenue and growth problems and some other issues that they typically have. But in this chapter, we want to talk about what we consider the driver of just about all of the outcomes of the company, basically, we want to talk about what's called (what we call) "The Marketing Problem".

When you first talk to companies these days, they may have an existing, well-defined sales process, if they are lucky. It may or may not be working very well for them. But they always have a marketing problem.

Contacts

And the problem is that first off, they have some sort of contact data[18] that's usually stored in multiple locations. It can be excel spreadsheets, it can be on clipboards, it can be on sticky notes, it can just be a bundle of business cards or it can be in access databases. [But the bottom line is, they don't have one central contact database.

Now what does that mean?

Let me give you a prime example.

[18.] In one instance, a major HVAC customer had 34000 Customer Records, but essentially zero emails.

My brother was on a call a with a SAP recruiter and she had sent him an email. But on the phone, she could not actually pull up the email she had sent to him, or his resume nor the job requirements because she did not have everything in front of her on her CRM.

This is a classic, classic symptom of a contact database management problem. But at least she had a contact.

For many companies, they don't have contacts. They haven't bothered to collect the names. I'll give you an example. We recently took on a client that said they had 34,000 contacts[19]. Unfortunately, only about 1,500 of them had some sort of email. The rest of them, well, they did not have any email addresses for those contacts. They had not bothered to collect email addresses over the years; I guess they just did not think of it. As a result, they said "oh what do you recommend? We were thinking about paying this service to append email addresses to it." So they did.

Unfortunately, the email service, despite a very large fee, was only able to associate about 7,500 contacts with an email. That's a lot but that is nowhere near 34,000 contacts.

What does this mean to you?

Prospects, Companies, Industry

Well, all those years, all those people? They really hadn't created a contact database. But for many companies, it is not just contact management that is a problem. They want to know who's visited them and what companies

---

[19]   Ibid

they are doing business with. Many can't currently do this today. Due to new regulations, such as the European GDPR directive, U.S. CAN-SPAMM Act, Know Your Customer Laws and many others, information that was once easily accessible to the marketing department is now encrypted, meaning you can't get to it unless you have special IT systems. This situation will continue to get worse as we go forward and governments around the world attempt to fix 'data privacy' issues.

What's the big deal?

How's Your Online Presence

Well, I am here to tell you that your website is your number one source of people finding you and your business. It would be great if you had the right system in place where you could see not just the fact that a visit occurred or what search term or channel they used to find you, but who they were, what company they were visiting from and what they were looking for.

But a lot of if not most people, unless they implemented the right solution, and that solution can vary, they really don't know that information. So their sales team is being starved to death for leads by marketing.

Bottom line.

If you have got an expensive sales team and if marketing isn't delivering the amount of contacts and the number of qualified leads they need, then between the 2 teams, marketing and sales, they really aren't aligned.

We will talk about this issue and how to correct it a little later on. Without this alignment between the 2 teams, they are not going to achieve their goals.

That's the marketing problem. It's quite complex. It's growing more complex all the time, and the very survival of your company depends on you getting this right to solve this problem. Marketing should be one of your company's primary revenue channels.

Are You Experiencing the Information Explosion Problem

The information explosion,[20] is, of course, not a new thing. What we want to talk about today are really 2 specific aspects of it that we've seen our customers suffer from.

Deals and Pipeline Management

One is trying to answer the question "what is in my pipeline visibility" which is a huge problem and the second one is the "pipeline data problem". They are related, but they are quite different and they both have similar solutions.

[20.] https://www.forbes.com/sites/bernardmarr/2018/05/21/how-much-data-do-we-create-every-day-the-mind-blowing-stats-everyone-should-read/

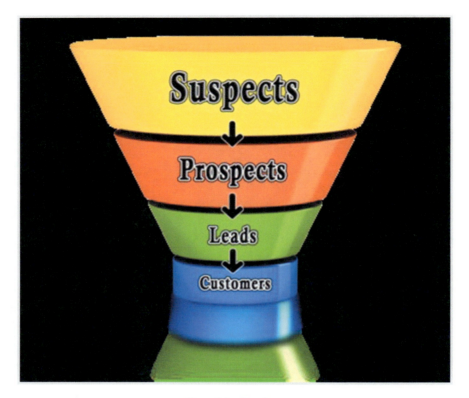

Your Sales Pipeline

But the pipeline visibility problem touches many areas of your business. For example, if I went to most companies today and asked, "what deals do you have in your pipeline"? They would be hard pressed to provide an answer, accurate or otherwise. For most, especially smaller firms, it would be almost impossible. I have worked for very large companies, where I 'owned' a sales pipeline. These companies had implemented state of the art ERP systems. They had state-of-the-art data warehouses and sales management systems and the bottom line is, no single person could really say what deal value was in the pipeline nor what the true probability was of closing any of the deals. At best, they were guessing as to the deal value, probable close dates and probability of closing it at all within any given time frame.

I will say this, the German ERP software company where I worked before had a pretty good idea about their own pipeline, but yet the place was overrun with spreadsheets and you know spreadsheets lead to spreadsheet hell.

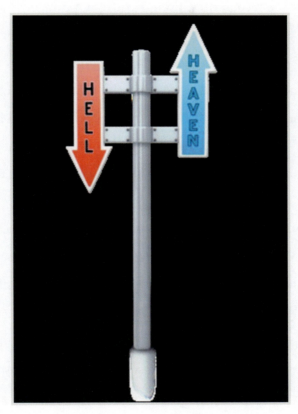

Spreadsheets Lead to the Hell of Bad Data

Financials

The second problem are the financials. If you don't know what's in your pipeline, you don't know if you have enough in your pipeline to meet your sales and revenue growth targets, therefore, it has got a severe financial impact on you. Not knowing your financials can lead to severe problems with sales forecasting. If you're publicly traded, and some of our clients have already become publicly traded, you have to follow very strict guidelines regarding revenue recognition. Even if you're not publicly traded, you still need to be able to forecast your revenue.

What we find is that small startup firms tend to be operating month-to-month, and are mostly focused on selling as much as possible, though they rarely know how much that should be. Once a firm makes it past about the three-million-dollar annual revenue mark, they should be setting a sales target and then working to it. Admittedly, they should be operating this way from the beginning, but it is not realistic.

For my clients in the three hundred to five hundred thousand dollar annual revenue range and up, they usually have an established sales track record, and therefore know about how much they will make a month. However, their finances do not usually allow them to set a sales target and then work backwards to the individual parts of the business to determine, for example, the required advertising spend.

For my larger clients, where they may have many products and services, they have a huge resource management problem to contend with. They may have thousands of field sales people all generating leads and pursuing deals. To do this and win, they need a huge number of highly qualified and expensive sales support and delivery resources to support the sales process. This invariably means they don't have the resources they need as and when needed, so they reach out to partners. That demand, created by marketing, just got wasted. This is both an IT Systems and Sales Discipline problem.

Tasks and Who Called

But it gets even worse; most people don't know what are the tasks they have committed to or should commit to to keep the pipeline actually flowing. Without the right level of pipeline visibility, you may not know if you have deals in your pipeline at all. If you don't have the right sales management systems in place, how do you answer questions like who called, what calls did or should I be making, what calls have I made, who have I sent emails to?

Contact Activity History

When I drill down a little further into any one of my typical customer's operations, if they don't have the right system in place, I usually find out they don't really have any activity history on their contacts. That doesn't sound like a big deal but you know the sales force typically has a pretty high turnover rate; if not the highest in the company, it will come pretty close. If you don't have a centralized solution to the pipeline and contact management system, when that salesperson walks out your door, all the investment that you made in establishing the relationship between the company and that sales guy walks out the door with them and if it is not in your activity record, guess what?

It's gone.

But you know, that's just one part of this huge problem.

Meetings

Any kind of meetings that you have had or which are scheduled are probably not being properly tracked in your system. In fact, it is very common to see companies where some meetings are scheduled in one system and some meetings are scheduled in another system. There are calendars that aren't really synching and meetings, frankly speaking, are amazingly expensive. They tie up a lot of people's time. They usually aren't very well organized. They don't have an agenda. Unless you are really diligent about it, most of the time they go far beyond what they were supposed to do in terms of time and there is no real follow up to them. In short, meetings[21] are the great time waster and you ought to be tracking them if you want to improve their effectiveness.

Deal Timelines

The other thing is that most companies don't have good visibility into their deals, which means they still don't really have visibility on the deal time line. You know, if you are working at a very sophisticated level, most of the time, you will be working with your client to actually work out a deal close plan.

On very complex sales, this becomes absolutely crucial because you have to make investment decisions in the sales process. Even for a small guy just going out for that daily Starbucks based client meeting, you still have to plan that out.

---

[21]   Steven R. Cover, "The 7 Habits of Highly Effective People: Powerful Lessons in Personal Change", 2004

Sales Funnel

Many companies have a problem just simply setting up, establishing and measuring a sales funnel. These days, it's in vogue to define the sales funnel as a flywheel, which is not wrong, just hard to model in a Sales Dashboard, never mind keep up-to-date. Within the world of complex IT systems, of which I have sold millions of dollars worth, you see what the real challenges are with defining your Sales Funnel. - Customers define their own way of buying, and it is often times designed to defeat your attempt to sell a certain way, particularly if you are trying to sell based on value.

Stalled Sales Process

Without all these elements in place, it's very hard to recognize when you have a stalled sales process. Now you have a bigger problem because sales management doesn't really know where or how it can intervene with its sales team to help them out.

Now you have sales talent going to waste, you don't have visibility into the problem and you don't have a system to help you through it. But there is even more.

You would think the information explosion problem would be making your data better, but that is not the case.

Bad Data Cost YOU Money

At the top of the list of impacts the information explosion is causing most businesses is that bad data is costing them money. It has been reported for many years now that the US is estimated to lose $600 billion dollars a year due to bad data. We call it the data quality problem, which is a subset of the overall Information Explosion problem.

Its impact really falls into 2 major areas. One's called the accuracy of the data and the other is called its staleness. How long has it been in your system? And just to kind of give you a data point here, it is estimated that between 25 and 40% of all the contacts in your email database will expire or die every year. So which ones have expired? Have you checked your data quality? Have you cleaned it up.

I had mentioned in a previous chapter the example of a recruiter calling and not being able to call up the resume that they were calling my brother about. They have applicant tracking systems or ATS'. Presumably, they would have it under control, but nope. An ATS without a CRM is going to leave you hanging.

But the sales pipeline data quality problem that goes into this has many little players, you know, fireman bucket brigades. One of the worst offenders or causes is everybody relying on Excel. Now excel is a great tool, it's been around for 25 or 30 years, maybe more, I've personally been using it most every day of my adult life both in business and in my personal life. I have seen it do many things.

But any time I have seen a company try to use it as a database or as their central contact management or sales pipeline management process, what I inevitably find is that it is inaccurate, it can't be maintained and it always, always leads to data being replicated over and over again. Like an alien, each replication has a slight mutation in it. It's basically a Darwinian evolution system and what you get is multiple versions of the truth, which means you actually have no version of the truth.

Sticky Notes Are Not Your Friend

The Japanese are big on using sticky notes. Sticky notes on the wall; they are very good for some problems. The problem is, it's hard to share a sticky note with your team mates half way across the world. In addition, they fall off the wall; they depend upon your hand writing quality; you really can't maintain the integrity of the data that you are putting on them. So not a great solution to the information explosion problem.

Nothing Written Down

But at least they are written down. In many organizations, there's nothing written down or there is very little written down. There are no standards about it. Let's be honest, if you have to write it down, if it takes too much work, especially on the sales side, they are notorious for not writing it down because that is not making them money or at least that is their attitude.

The problem is, is if it's not written down and it is not automatically recorded, in other words, you haven't put a system in place that makes that sort of happen automatically, you are losing an awful lot of information that you will find is costing you money down the road.

Not Measurable

But it also leads to other problems, such as nothing is measurable. If it's not written down, and it is not in a system where you can actually collect data from it, you really can't measure anything. You don't know how many deals are in your pipeline. You don't know what they are worth. You don't know what they are worth because you don't have standards as far as when you record your deal value. That's why one of my and many other sales manager's recommendations is and I personally believe this, is that when you put a deal in the pipeline, put in the expected value of the deal. If you don't do this, you cannot do probability weighted deal forecasting.

Not only that, sometimes there is intentional bad data. How many deals close the last day of the quarter or the last day of the month? Well, it could be due to simple old laziness. It is also intentional. It is not unusual for a guy who has a quota, once he's made it, and he's a little bit over it, to have put something in his pocket and slow it down regardless of the impact on the company. Not saying it happens to you, but it is a possibility. But I am saying it happens, I've seen it and I have been impacted by it.

But all that data that's in your pipeline - there is another problem, it costs money to manage. And most companies, unless they are a big company, let's face it, they are not really investing a lot of money to manage their data.

We are going to show you how we think that you can automate most of this data management problem. But you also have to have systems and procedures in place as well as sales discipline to automate most of these problems out of existence.

Summary

Without all these systems, what do you get? You get stalled sales processes and sometimes you recognize these processes as stalled and sometimes you don't.

The Sales Team Problem.

Now, sales is not a problem. Sales is actually an outcome. But we've yet to find a company that doesn't really have a problem with either their sales team or their sales process.

Where Did That Sale Come From?

What you should know is sales, they just don't fall into your lap. The competition out there for every dollar is fierce. In fact, in 2008, whereas you had about 5 suppliers for any product or service, by 2016, you had between 14 and 16 suppliers for these same products and services. This means you are facing about 3 times as much competition as you were facing just 10 years ago, according to Brian Halligan, CEO of Hubspot[22]. So what's the problem, what are we seeing out there?

[22.] Inbound 2016, Kick-Off Speech, Brian Halligan, CEO of Hubspot

<u>Brian Halligan, Keynote, Hubspot Inbound 2016</u>

Need to Track Outbound Sales Contacts

For many companies, perhaps they have been sold a bill of goods when it comes to sales. Perhaps what has emerged is that if the idea of we're just going to get everybody to walk in the front door and buy from us didn't quite work out, it did work somewhat. But what is very obvious for very complicated sales, the marketing team, once it gets leads to the sales team, the sales team now has to close the deal. In other words, outbound has not gone away and all the traditional skills of sales, relationship building, closing, speaking, you know, getting the contracts done, continue to be extremely important.

But what do we typically hear. Let's just go down the list. A lot of these should sound familiar to you. We've certainly heard them a number of times and we may have said a few a few times our selves.

Marketing Leads Are No Good

The first thing we are going to hear from a sales team is "Ah the marketing leads are no good". Well some are, some are not, but ultimately, the leads are the leads and it's up to sales to sell them.
Which leads us to a second problem, which is in today's business world, you know they are aware of lead scoring. They have not put much of a thought process into what that means exactly and it is kind of a vague thing. It is fairly complicated but bottom line is, that yes, companies want to score their leads, whatever that means to them but the meaning changes over time and the quality of the leads changes over time.

So marketing leads are no good. That's not really the main problem. You have either got an insufficient volume of high quality leads or you have got a weak sales process to take advantage of the leads that you have.

Sales Process

What does that mean. Well, let me give you a little bit of background. I once pursued a low qualified lead for *5 years*. Every week, I had to report to my boss on the status of this lead. Keep in mind, this was in the corporate world. My boss wanted to know why I was still pursuing this lead if they didn't have an RFP. And it was because I knew at the end of the day, these guys were going to buy from us. I had my own ways of doing it. But I knew the industry. I knew the client. I knew they had the budget. I just knew that they were very slow and we needed to just give them their space. But nevertheless, we had a process and the secret was we kind of sat down with them and we designed their selection process. And today, that is one of the largest customers of its type in the world.

Of course, if you are small, you can't afford 5 years on pre-sales. But if you are a large enterprise, this whole thing of disqualifying them early, I take that with a grain of salt, that is my personal opinion on that but my personal opinion is backed by my own experience.

What is the other problem with the sales team?

Weak Closing Process

If you have a defined sales process you have probably spent a lot of money developing it. What you will find is most of your sales people probably aren't following it like you expected and you don't have a very good way to track it. Some of this is due to a lack of a system and some of it is due to management problems. Then, frankly speaking, some sales teams have a closing issue. Sometimes, it is a skills problem. Sometimes, it's a problem of no one has really sat down and engineered the whole process end-to-end and provided them with sales enablement documents and tools.

What Does That Mean?

Well, one of the impacts of not having done that is it is routine to see a sales person preparing his own content to close a deal. I kid you not, I have seen them spend 24 hours of continuous effort to write contracts that somebody else could have easily done. That is time that they were not closing, they were not working the next deal and were not really utilizing their time appropriately.

Is it Avoidable?

Yes, it is. You have to think through how can I take that off his plate such that sales is not producing additional content on their own. Let's face it, a sales contract is a piece of marketing content that the marketing team could prepare and make look more professional. The sales team's job is to close sales. The contractual process has to be engineered into your system so you know and can measure and manage your system.

The other problem is that a lot of sales teams have all these wonderful tools that tell you basically a thousand times more about any particular contact than they would ever know before. Yet they are not taking the time to do the research to uncover the information that is readily available to them.

For example, if I am in marketing and I give you a contact to work, one of your first actions should be to look up that contact on LinkedIn. You would be shocked at how many sales people are not putting that resource to good use.

You Have More Information Than You Think

But with the systems that are available out there today, it is entirely possible that a company itself, inside its own systems, knows a lot about contacts but because of all the other problems that they have got, a sales person is not able to actually access all that information so that they can be a more effective sales person. Lack of access is also a problem that most sales people run into. It is usually caused by the IT department imposing restrictions that should not be imposed. But the Sales Managers do not take the time to fight that battle.

What Sales Activity Do I Prioritize?

The other problem is the sales people and sales teams are struggling with setting priorities. They don't know whether to do prospecting, they don't know whether to focus just on closing the deal, they don't know what it is going to take to meet quota, or even if they have a quota, in short, they are suffering from multiple priorities, faulty systems design, skills issues and staff turnover and they are under tremendous pressure.

The Multi-System, IT Patchwork Mess Problem

So in this chapter, we decided to come up with the really catchy name for the problem called "The Multi-System, IT Patchwork Mess Problem."

Just What Does That Mean?

Well, can you answer this question? How many existing systems do you have or subscribe to in your enterprise? You might be shocked to find out just how many things that you are consuming these days.

Let's Get Down to Brass Tacks Here

Is someone else managing your website? Do you even know what that means?
We've run across a number of companies where they have been paying a substantial fee, usually to an overseas company, to manage their website. And when you ask the question "well, what exactly does that mean?", you usually find no one really knows for sure. I mean if the website is hosted on Godaddy for example, Godaddy is in charge of making sure it runs. So the short answer is, their tasks are undefined, their deliverables are undefined, but as long as the website is up, the owner is happy. It's not generating any leads for them. It's not helping them make any sales. And it's probably not actually having anything done to it from one month to the next and if it does fall over, there is no system out there telling you what is going on.

So, if you have a maintenance problem with your website and it's a big complex beast, perhaps you have an underlying systems problem. But there is an awful lot of money flowing out of your business, in all likelihood, for people who aren't really doing anything for you and since they have no performance metrics or deliverables to meet, are not delivering value to you. You are probably short changing some people and problems where you could be putting a little bit more money.

Multiple Subscriptions

The bottom line is you have a lot of systems, and they each have their particular quirks that are affecting you.

Time Suck and Money Suck

All of them together are a massive time suck to manage. There is just no getting around it. They are also a huge money suck. They don't run on their own. And all these cloud based systems have their subscription fees. Those subscription fees tend to climb over time and pretty soon you have a substantial outflow of cash each month. Even if you don't go that route and you buy the systems outright, you are still going to spend a lot of money on them.

But even if you spend all that money to buy all these capabilities, there is another problem that we commonly see. What is it?

Accessibility Problem, AKA Security

Now, again, I come out of the corporate world and there were many days when my blood pressure got quite high because I didn't have authorization to see what I needed to see to do my job. And the answer is always the same from the IT wonks "well tell me what you need it for"?

By the time I do that, the need or the idea or the impetus for doing it, has already passed. So, if you got a hyper restricted system and you got people who can't get to what they need to get to, here is what actually happens "*they stop trying to access it*".
So the security part is fine, but the actual reason for the systems existence is utterly defeated.

Data Quality Problem

Along with the system access problem, you have a data quality problem. Some data quality problems are caused by users putting in bad data but most of the time the data quality problems are caused by the systems themselves not being properly designed to prevent bad data from seeping in, in the first place.

Look Deeper

But it is a little bit deeper than that. Just getting the data correctly into a field doesn't mean you've actually solved your data quality problems. Often times, you didn't collect the right information in the first place. Now you have a data quality problem but of a whole different nature.

You Can't Handle the Multiple Truth

Well, one of the most common problems that it leads to is what is called the "multiple versions of the truth problem". This simply means the more dispersed your organization is, the more versions of the truth exist. There is just no way around this. The bigger the organization is, the more often this happens. But even one man shows can often times have an internal two man view of a particular problem.

How Does This Happen?

Sometimes, it's because data gets lost. A common scenario is, two of your sales people are working on one client [and they both create deals about the client because the systems aren't in place to help manage the problem], you now end up with deals about the same client from 2 different people in your company and you don't know how much you've got at stake there.
There's a lot of side effects from that sort of setup.

What's That Stale I Smell?

But the other problem is, is that systems that are not easily accessed, that are not actively maintained, data sort of starts to die in there. Old data goes there and just kind of fades away. Sometimes this old data is very valuable.

For example, a large retailer that I know that has a lifetime return policy literally keeps a record of every transaction that anybody has ever made in that store [for the lifetime of their membership]. [And you can pull up 20 years' worth of data on any single customer.] For that company, that data is very, very valuable. The problem is that, it is also very expensive; it's time consuming to maintain but it is commercially very attractive for them to be able to hold that kind of data on a client.

But for most businesses, really what they need is Data that is accurate and current as of this minute.

You Have to Design for That.

There are other systems that you are also using that are outside your domain but most assuredly are connected to your domains and by domains I don't mean just your website. We are going to talk about that a little bit and how they have an impact of on you.

One of the biggest external systems out there is called "google pay per click advertising".

So just about every website out there either has or should have google analytics tracking code installed on it. It sounds so simple - copy this code, paste it in and you are done. But when you get into the details what you typically find is it is not really installed fully or correctly and there are a thousand different people with a thousand different opinions about what you should be doing. Now the good thing about it is, if you get to the right ad spend level you can actually get google on the phone, which we do all the time and they will kind of give you their over-the-shoulder best practice advice.

Now, that said, I can take you to any number of PPC providers and they will always say "Yeah google will always tell you what to do to spend more money in their system".

That may or may not be true but bottom line is, if I can get google to help me or you then I am going to do it. But is not a simple task to fully set it up and a whole lot of people make a whole lot of money helping companies optimize that and your's may or not be fully optimized.

There is another kind of google advertising system called Google PLA, or Product Listing Ads, that are pretty simple to set up but to truly optimize them and take advantage of the artificial intelligence capabilities that exist out there, you really have to get into them and they don't work well on their own if your website and your products are not fully optimized in and of themselves.

So people tend to think it's one and done but because the systems have an end-to-end relationship even when they cross boundaries you have to get all the parts right to get full business value out of them.

And Facebook has the same issue. You can sell on Facebook. Facebook itself has an e-commerce capability most people are not very good at using. Facebook has as many ad types as google does.

But it has an underlying logic that is slightly different. Now we know Facebook currently has some controversies in terms of the data access but the bottom line is, for some companies that get it right, Facebook is an incredibly effective advertising channel and you can prove it while other companies that don't get it right have come away and said it's not working for me. It's kind of hard to ignore the channel that has 2 billion users. There has just never been anything in human history that has had that level of access to so many people.

So Facebook, it's there, they will work through whatever problems they have, it's going to keep improving, the cost is going to keep going up but if you don't have any sales from these efforts none of this really matter, right.

The No Sales Problem.

We've seen it many times where companies have a whole bunch of irons in the fire but the sales aren't working and this is leading to huge issues for them. The sales were working, they've stopped. Competitors have taken their market share.

And so, the question you always have to ask yourself is "so why is it working for others and not for me?"

That is a sure sign that something is probably not working in your approach to using these different channels. Just think about all the channels that exist out there that are potential digital marketing and sales channels. You got Facebook and you got google, you've also got twitter, of course, you know the Commander in Chief lives on twitter. You've got Pinterest, in Europe you've got xing, and any number of other social media networks that all are trying to help you do the same thing; they are all there to bring people together and if they're the channel that's right for your market, you are going to have to master it.

One of the other ones that you know you need to think about is Bing, the Microsoft one, it actually is a very effective channel for many people. Instagram, owned by Facebook, is actually a better channel for consumer goods in our experience than Facebook itself. But because they go together they are highly integrated.

In the B2B world your main player is LinkedIn. But that is not to say that Facebook doesn't also work very well for you.

There are other systems that we see that bring complexity to your life such as other CRM's, for example. Many people use Salesforce as that's the leader, but Salesforce is only one of many, many CRM's and they all have their issues, they bring their own level of complexity and you have to think through it. How am I going to use this, what is the best way, because honestly, they can all suck up every minute of every day and you will not make your sale.

And Then Video.

Video at this point is really the way to drive traffic. You got the big player, Youtube.

But you have a whole host of other video platforms, each of which has its purpose in life.

And then finally, you have TV advertising that also comes with its own systems implications. Many, many systems are required to get TV ad spend feeding back into your own system and measuring the impact and improving the impact.

But there are systems[23] out there that integrate with your marketing platforms that are available and they all have a cost and they all contribute to the multi-system mega IT system mess that exists at each company.

Welcome to the Human Resources Problem.

Now I hate to call it the human resources problem, but given the extreme importance of you getting the right people on the bus as they say, we wanted to devote a special chapter to this. There's a lot to unpack in the whole right people on the bus approach. First off, you have to have the bus. That means, you, the business owner, have to have thought deeply about what you're offering to the market. When this is clear, the people problem will start to come more into focus.

---

[23] CallRail, for instance, allows you to track Inbound Telephone Calls specifically given out during TV Commercials. You can also monitor call activity in real time on Google Analytics with this system installed.

Who's Going to Do The Work?

What we are actually seeing out there, especially in the digital marketing space, as well as the sales assistant space is a tendency to put the intern on it. The least qualified person in your company who may not even be in your company is typically a student. You may have a highly defined sales and marketing process, with highly trained people in each role. We rarely see this. Instead, and especially within marketing teams, given that much of what they are asked to do these days is perceived as sort of new, i.e., selling on social media, we see the intern or the newest guy in the door get assigned this duty.

That's not working. What is working is what has always worked. Defining the job, broadly speaking, hiring the best people you can find, then training and mentoring them to suit your requirements.

Usually the[24] most Least Interested

Though not always the case, an intern is usually not nearly as interested in your businesses success as you are. They are there to learn, not to lead. Yet, in case after case, we've encountered interns being delegated the authority and responsibility to develop marketing plans, do sales, and meet with technology vendors. This almost never works out well. You will never know though until the intern is gone.

---

24.   Most college curriculums are at least 10 years behind where current technology is.

Most Disinterested Person Put in Charge to Run Your Business Growth Plan

This intern is often times being tasked with the thing that will help you achieve your sales and revenue goal. We just don't think that is the best strategy going forward. They have the least amount of experience, they are the least trained and it is great that you are training them up. But it is just far too important these days to be letting your marketing efforts be done by the least qualified person.

Growth Strategy

That is why you need to have a clear growth strategy. By growth, we mean both revenue for the company as well as the size of the team and systems to support your growth plan. By quantifying your growth strategy, meaning putting a stake down on getting to that revenue target, you can begin to define concrete plans and action to achieving your goals.

This is by far one of the most difficult and complex task that any business has to perform. Yet, in this author's experience with very large companies, they achieve success because they planned to achieve success. The opposite is also true, for many smaller clients, unfortunately, the growth plan is simply to keep the doors open one more day. That's no way to run a ship.

Marketing

Marketing people with the skillsets to thrive in today's high tech marketing landscape are in short supply. You will most likely either have to hire and train or pay a lot more for contractors than you've ever paid in the past. This is only going to get worse.

Hire Good Help. Not the Cheapest You Can Find

It's very much the case that marketing used to be at least the second highest paid position in the company. What we are seeing is that the skills demanded by these positions are just exploding.

You have to be able to write, be culturally aware, digitally aware and have mastery of many, many pieces of technology which they will not have learned in college, even if a recent graduate. We are not talking being able to write code, although that is helpful. We are talking really just core fundamental skills across a variety of platforms, with industry background preferably.

This kind of puts you in the realm of needing people that are much higher up the skills ladder and thus usually much more expensive. It does not make a whole lot of sense to be investing in very expensive systems and have very expensive sales and marketing growth goals if you don't have the right people.

The No Budget Problem

Let's talk about the no budget problem.

Everybody wishes that this could be done for cheap and by this, I mean marketing and sales but marketing in particular.

Would You Like To Solve Your Problems

Let's be honest - would you like to solve your marketing and sales problems?

Get Ready for Sticker Shock

Well, let me tell you, it's time to get ready for sticker shock because everything about marketing is getting more expensive. there is just no way around this. It's hyper competitive and they are not raising their prices, it's just that everybody is trying to use the same channels and the same mechanisms and so there is a supply and demand problem for ad space on channels like Facebook.

But what does all this lead to and what do we see?

Unrealistic Expectations: Never Had to Spend This Much Before

Especially among the smaller companies we take on board. They really have unrealistic expectations of what they are going to have to spend on marketing. Even some of the larger companies, even though they are doing well revenue wise, perhaps their revenue is flat and yet, a very common refrain we still hear is "well we have never had to spend this much before".

A Successful Growth Plan Plan is Neither Cheap Nor Free

And let's face it, what we are really talking about here is that you are probably looking at 50 to 100 thousand dollars just for one marketing platform per year. This is in addition to ad spend and that will get you some services but not all. So the one man store, yeah they can still start, they can still exist but realistically, you need 100 K or more to invest if you want to do a million in revenue, it is just flat out the way it is. So what you should take away from the no budget problem is, is that a successful growth plan is neither cheap nor free and you have to pay for it. There is just no question about it.

It's Quite Expensive In Terms of Money and Time

That said, of course, all the business and IT systems have to be in place. All that costs money, strategies have to be in place, that costs money, creative has to be in place, paid advertising has to be in place, and you have to have the systems in place, well-engineered, structured, tested and exercised to make use of all this data and this leads to a need for a very large budget on both the marketing and sales side.

No Past Experience[25]

For many companies, whether new or established, they do not have experience with these new types of cloud based systems. Perhaps they are fortune 500 class companies and have had SAP implemented for years. Those systems were and are very expensive to purchase and implement. Now, along comes a system like Hubspot,

---

25.   Most businesses will have many IT systems. A small startup business owner will typically have to identify, select, purchase, install and integrate all of the various systems on their own.

available in the cloud only. It doesn't cost anywhere near as much as a 50 user SAP license would cost. But the cost will start to add up, and you will soon need other systems.

Don't Know How Many Leads It Takes to Creata a Customer

During my almost 20 years of SAP consulting experience, I led or participated in over 150 SAP Pre-Sales engagements, where I noticed one thing in particular – the assumption that a company already had a large customer base and large number of contacts. Along with that, it was 'assumed' that they understood their conversion funnels.

The truth is, that was rarely the case. Much of the sales process was and is completely disconnected from the marketing process. The systems just were not designed at a time when it was possible to know everything about everybody at every stage of the process. This means that few if any companies truly know how many leads it takes to create a customer.

No Idea of the Marketing Spend Required to Generate Enough Leads to Generate Enough Customers

If you're trying to budget for marketing, and you don't know how many leads you have to generate to generate a customer, you going to have a huge problem estimating how much you will have to spend to generate not just a customer, but enough customers.

What is Your Marketing Spend as a Percent of Revenue X%

A typical approach to budgeting for marketing spend has been to budget based on a percent of revenue. Not a bad approach, if all you want is some high-level macro number. But unacceptable as an approach when you are continuously being forced to adjust budgets based on consumer behavior, which is now possible in real time. The real answer is how much can you afford to spend as long as you're profitable.

Are You Willing to Spend X% to Reach Your Sales Growth Goals?

For many mid-size companies, who are wanting to grow sales rapidly, they are going to have to make painful decision as to how much they are willing to spend on marketing in order to hit their sales goals. This number is often large and unstable.

Unaware of the Rising Cost of all the Channels

For most companies, we have found they are simply unaware of the ever-rising cost of most advertising channels. The cost of Google and Facebook seem to be rising rapidly as well as most other digital channels. That's because they work and are extremely competitive. The amount of spend required to make these channels work is usually shocking to most companies.

Google Attacking Angie's List and Homeadvisor

There is no channel or market that is not experiencing disruption from Google. Angie's list is one of those channels. Google has aggressively targeted it and other sites just like it with their own competing services. We expect this behavior to continue, industry by industry. For you, the businessman, it means you're going to have to spend on nearly perfect content and SEO, as well as have the right systems in place to withstand the onslaught.

Google Monopolization Leads to Price Increases

Having by far the largest share of the search market space, Google has near monopoly pricing power. Here's the thing, they don't actually set the prices, the auction sets the price. You and other businesses are essentially setting the price when you bid to hit the number one position on Google. They make money regardless but do seem to want their users to have a good experience. By good experience, they mean achieving their search goal. This will only get worse as the Google Search Algorithm[26] advances.

Never Spent Money Before to Create Content. It's Expensive

For many companies, they have little if any marketing ready content. If you are a startup, as many of our smaller customers are, a brochure may be all you have. Even those can cost a lot of money to produce. Yes, the process for getting a simple 3 fold, color brochure has been greatly simplified by technology. However, if

---

26. Google states publicly that they implement about 3500 changes to their search algorithm annually.

you're not able to design it yourself, the complete cost of even a simple brochure can rise into the thousands with printing cost.

Little Guy Thinks Something is Going to Happen for Free

For the small business owner, there often is no explicit budget set aside for such things as content production or sales enablement. This leads to an unwillingness to experiment or try out new systems or platforms. i.e., interactive content.

If I Could Give You a System That Solves Most Of Your Problems And Knocks It Out Of The Park and It's a 10, What Would Do Next?

What if I told you all of these problems, including: Strategy, Budget, Human Resources, Marketing, Sales and Information Technology, have a solution? The truth is, it is possible that with a well thought out, well-funded approach, you can achieve success. In the next chapter, I am going to walk you through the solution(s) for each of these problems.

CHAPTER THREE

SOLUTIONS

The Solution

In the first section of this book, I laid out all the problems a business faces across all functional areas of its business, rather than just taking a narrow view of marketing and sales. Now we are going to do a deep dive into how you solve these same problems using the right combination of technology, strategy and tactics.

How Does Hubspot Help You Solve These Problems

Growth Plan

We mentioned in Chapter One that if you're aren't growing, you're dying. If your business is stable, meaning your revenue is the same from one year to the next, you're also dying, just at a slower rate. That's why just about all companies need a growth plan, usually around a term known within the Balanced Scorecard Strategy Management community, as a quantified vision. In simple terms, it means putting down a revenue goal that reflects a realistic goal, say to grow the business from 5 million in annual revenue to 6 million in annual revenue, which would be a 20% annual growth rate.

When you have such a specific, measurable, quantified, realistic, time bound revenue goal, you can break it down into monthly revenue targets, and within a system like Hubspot, embed those revenue goals within your CRM system. You also happen to have a SMART goal, which stands for Specific, Measurable, Attainable, Realistic and Time Bound, which is what the marketing world likes to call them.

How would that look like? $6,000,000 a year works out to be $500,000 a month in revenue. Let's say your Sales Process is somewhat complicated and the typical Sales Representative is tasked with delivering $1,000,000 a year in revenue in order to hit his Quota[27]. That would mean you need 6 Sales Representatives, at a minimum, to hit your Annual Revenue Target and you would use your Hubspot CRM to set a monthly quota per rep of $83,333.

Evaluate Your Goals

So let's walk through the above scenario and see if it is truly SMART? Is it specific, yes, you want to hit $6,000,000 a year in revenue. Is it measurable? Absolutely, and in the most relevant terms, revenues. Is it attainable? It may be, but you won't know that until all the other elements of the planning process have been

---

[27]   You could further refine this calculation with the use of AOV or Average Order Value.

done. Is it realistic? It may be, but it will require substantial investment to achieve. Is this investment realistic for the company's financial means? Finally, is it time bound? Yes, it is a one year target.

What Do You Sell and How Do You Sell It?

This may seem like a fairly 'dumb' question, but would that it were. First, a bit of background about the Author's business and digital marketing journey using Hubspot. Our company, SAP BW Consulting, Inc. has been in existence since 2008, while the author has been implementing SAP since 1999, preceded by nearly 30 years of military logistics and IT experience. This past experience also included starting a couple of other companies either of my own or as branches of existing businesses.

When we launched our business, we were focused on selling SAP BW Consulting. We did OK, and eventually we were invited to become partners of Hubspot, which is why, today, we mostly provide Inbound Marketing services to SAP Partners and Customers and a variety of other related enterprises.

What We Should Have Done

We should have 'productized our services'. What does that mean? We should have developed a service offering that was easily understood and consumed by our clients. What we do in the SAP space is typically done on-site, with some off-site work possible. When we became Hubspot partners, they provided us with what was essentially a business-in-a-box model, much like McDonalds provides an operator's manual for franchisees. Though we have sold several million dollars worth of projects, we could have and intend to sell much more.

The Takeaway.

We know, from experience, to start all Inbound Marketing engagements by understanding our client's product or service as well as their sales process. As a SAP Project Manager, who is certified in implementing SAP projects using what is known as SAP ASAP or AcceleratedSAP (recently renamed SAP Activate), a project management tool which maps to the Project Management Institutes (PMI) Project Management Professional (PMP) system, my 'productized service' was leading a SAP Project from scratch using the SAP ASAP methodology.

The SAP ASAP methodology is actually part of a larger framework called the Customer Engagement Lifecycle, or CEL. The CEL defines the activities and deliverables during all phases of the typical SAP customer lifecycle. This includes everything that comes before, during and after the implementation. After having lead the implementation of a large number of SAP projects, all of which were successful, I learned a thing or two.

The SAP ASAP methodology is a productized service. It consisted of a large number of specific deliverables with defined delivery standards. It defines both customer and consultant responsibilities and it relies on several tools, such as the SAP Solution Manager. It is path dependent, meaning the initial conditions, as established by the project manager, largely determine (but not totally), the success or failure of the project.

For any client who wants to dominate their market using digital marketing, productizing your offering will be a key to success. In addition, designing a high performance, digitally enabled sales funnel, will be an absolutely critical element of success. So how can Hubspot help with this process?

Hubspot is a Measurement System

Though many tools out there provide measurement, such as Google Analytics, none come close to providing the valuable insight delivered by Hubspot.

What Does Hubspot Help Us Measure?

- **Sales We Make** – Without exception, every company we have worked with, both within the Hubspot space as well as SAP, has had problems actually determining who they made a sale too. Some even struggle to define what a customer is. Let me help you out on this one – they bought something from you. Who doesn't know this information? Retailers, mostly. If you buy from them in cash, they have no idea who you are. They used to not care. Now they do. Amazon certainly does.

- **Contacts we have** – Hubspot relies heavily on having an email to identify contacts. On the sales side, it will allow you to create contacts without emails. But then how do you contact them? The bigger issue is typically that contacts are, in fact, stored all over the place. Hubspot provides both a central contact database as well as a view of everything that contact has done on your website and an ability to respond to that activity.

- **Leads to Prospects to Customers Sales Funnel Measurements** – Hubspot provides a view of you Sales Funnel as its 'first view' for marketing and sales. It also provides a measurement in percentage terms, between each stage of your Sales Funnel. Though some clients have been disappointed by how poorly their existing sales funnel actually converts, without this information, there is little you can do to change it.

- **End-to-End by Channel** - Hubspot provides the ability to measure your funnel performance by each channel, including Paid, Organic, Social, Referral, Direct and Tracking URLs. Partner products, all fully integrated into Hubspot, allow you to track webinar performance, TV ad performance, SMS performance, Event Performance, app performance, and many more.

Which Channels are Working Best?

Because it provides tracking by channel, you can tell which marketing channel is performing best. One obvious benefit is that it allows you to focus your advertising spend on high-performing channels and reduce spend on low performing channels. The real superpower here is that by combining both marketing and sales, you can determine which channel works best from a revenue perspective. This is critical if you want to keep marketing from generating a large number of poorly qualified leads.

Where Did The Contact Come From?

This is an area where Hubspot really shines – it can help you determine key information and insights about your contacts, such as:

- Company
- Region
- Interest

Which Online Content is Working Best?

This capability is especially useful given the cost of producing content, the overwhelming volume of content being produced everyday, by both marketing and sales and the shortage of people with the skills and knowledge to up your content game. Hubspot allows you to store and deliver content in a wide variety of formats, from whitepapers to calculators, both online and downloadable as well as videos.

The SLA Equation

The Service Level Agreement or SLA as it is known, is an agreement between Marketing and Sales that defines the responsibilities of each. Though there is a never ending zone of conflict between marketing and sales, the SLA forces both parties to commit to a revenue goal. This revenue goal needs to be completely aligned to the overall revenue target.

The Performance Metrics You Have to Hit to Achieve Your Growth Plan

By reversing the math on a top down Marketing and Sales Funnel view of things, you can determine how many visits marketing must generate to the company website, how many contacts must be obtained, how many of those must be converted into leads and eventually converted into Marketing Qualified Leads (MQLs), and how many of those need to be passed to sales. You can also determine how many MQLs must be accepted and converted into Sales Qualified Leads (SQLs), and of those, how many must be converted into customers.

We actually turned all of this into a simple, online calculator which takes your annual revenue target, your conversion rates between stages (if known) and determines this information for you. What we find is that most prospects, when they first come to us, do not know this information nor do they have the measurement systems in place.

Most business owners not only do not know this information, they are reluctant to establish it. This may because it is hard to do. It may be because it is politically difficult to do. But by installing the Hubspot tracking code you can quickly get the real information. Then, and only then, can you start to work on improving each stage of your sales funnel.

Once this measurement system is in place, it is also possible to assign a value to each lead. We've also developed an online calculator for this. It is based on work done by Mark Roberge in his book, The Sales Acceleration Formula.[28] To be clear, 100% of the time, business owners say a lead has zero value to them until it is converted into a customer. But that view won't help you solve your Growth and Revenue problem. This approach puts marketing on a revenue quota, something not possible until you get your SLA in place.

Your Marketing Team has a lot on its plate. If you want them to succeed, you first have to clearly define what you are selling and how you intend to sell it. We've already told you that Hubspot allows your marketing and sales team to enter into an SLA. But it goes way beyond this.

---

[28]. The Sales Acceleration Formula, Mark Roberge, 2015, Wiley Press

Central Contact Database – Your Digital Nervous System

Hubspot gives your Marketing Team an Integrated Tool that ties all the internal and external IT systems together. In this type of IT environment all of the data is always in alignment. This is also known as one version of the truth.

With this system, which allows marketing and sales to hold each other accountable with management oversight, you have complete visibility into:

- Contacts/People
- Prospects/Companies/Industry
- History/Location/Region
- Measurement of Your Online Presence
- All Contacts/and Activities on the Website
- Time Line for Contacts/Prospects/Company Information
- Who/Which Company/
- Products and Services You Sell
- Quotes
- Conversations
- Chatbot Interactions

Advanced E-Mail

It also comes with an Integrated Email System[29], which provides for behavior-based emails to be used in lead nurturing sequences.

Publishes Short Links to Social Media

It is designed to allow you to publishes short links to Social Media so people can publish information back to your site and you can track and monitor every interaction on your social media channels.

SEO Optimizers at Every Level of Your System

It provides SEO (Search Engine Optimization) Optimizers[30] at every level of your system. This part of the system alone makes it worthwhile. You don't have to use a huge number of non-integrated tools to come up with keyword information.

---

29. Email remains a highly effective marketing channel. For some e-commerce clients, we've seen 40% conversion rates on highly refined email lead nurturing sequences.
30. The optimizer evolves constantly to keep up with the demands of the constant changes being made by Google.

Content Strategy Tool Replaces Keyword Tool

When combined with the Content Strategy Tool, which incorporates the Keyword Tool, you can optimize not just every website page, blog page and landing page on your site, but every email and social media post as well. With its Artificial Intelligence (AI) and Machine Learning (ML) capabilities, the system is able to recommend phrases[31] to be added to your publicly facing web pages. These recommendations are based on what it has learned from 'user's intent', as displayed on other parts of your website, plus other data sources it has access to.

Competitor Analysis Tool

The competitor analysis tool is also very useful in helping you analyze your site's ranking as well as your competitors. We've found that it allows us to segment, analyze and target companies based on how competitive their website actually is. This is far different than just looking at a website and trying to be better than them. By looking at your competitors' backlinks, you can execute a sophisticated link building strategy by finding what each of your competitors are getting links for, and doing[32] it better.

---

31. It does a surprisingly good job of making recommendations as to phrases you should include in the text of your blogs. We find they are often spot on and industry specific.
32. Backlinks are links from other websites to your website. Backlinks are one of the SEO elements Google places emphasis on when ranking a website.

Back-Link Tool

With its built-in backlink tool, you can quickly see whether backlinks improve a sites ranking (spoiler alert, if they are high quality[33], yes, they do and we have extensive data on just how much it does).

Advertising ROI

In almost every business, paid advertising is part of the marketing mix. Though there are many, many different channels where you could spend your advertising dollars; it is highly likely you'll spend much of it on Google Pay Per Click (PPC) advertising. Each platform, such as Google or Facebook, comes with its own advertising platform, each of which requires the insertion and configuration of tracking codes. We'll discuss these aspects of advertising a little later on but for now, just know that setting up these codes and making adjustments is not a set it and forget it operation, despite constant improvements being made by each platform.

When you combine the complete visibility of the lead-to-cash cycle[34] that Hubspot provides with paid advertising, you can see which channel is actually working and the actual ROI of your advertising spend. There's a never ending battle going on between the platforms to both provide a better advertising platform while at the same time, restricting useful pieces of information from you, the marketer or business owner. This will not get better. The challenge is to setup your system, in most cases, a Hubspot platform, and connect it up to the various other platforms, then use the 'God's eye view' of how exactly each customer came to be

---

[33]. Backlinks normally have a 'quality rating' as defined by Google. It is reflective of the quality of the source website from whence the backlink came.

[34]. The lead-to-cash cycle measures how long it takes a prospect to become a lead known to your system and then get converted into a sale and result in cash collection.

a customer that Hubspot provides. Once you get this set up and working, then you have a system you can scale up quickly, dependent upon your delivery capability and advertising spend capability.

Though I've spoken mostly about Google PPC, the same holds true for Facebook, both of which platforms I've spent massive sums of advertising dollars on. Facebook, being a social platform, requires you to be, naturally enough, more social in your approach. This means doing more than just advertising your wares. People are looking for entertainment, even from vendors. There's lots you can do with this platform. You will continue to see a demand for 'social media' managers, and their price will rise. The challenge is making sure the ROI is there, visible, measured and then scaled. Prepare to spend a lot of money making this happen.

Solving For The Information Explosion Problem

All of these systems, including Hubspot, Salesforce, SAP, and a variety of connected systems, lead to one huge, ginormous, scary, problem. We call it the information explosion problem. You may see all kinds of 'hype' out there about the rate of knowledge doubling every year. But if you're trying to run a business, whether small, medium or large, you have data growing out of your ears.

Solving the Data Explosion Problem

This is manageable if you're a mid-sized firm, say with 1 or 2 marketers and 3 to 5 million in sales. But as you get bigger, and your deal volume increases, your data volume increases exponentially. In one of our clients, they were generating approximately 1,400 contacts a day, but there were some days when they were generating 27,000 contacts a day.

In addition, the client was running a major TV advertising campaign on a sustained basis which drove calls to a Salesforce Call Center, at a rate of several thousand calls an hour. All of this call activity was integrated into Hubspot, which is a simple process.

But as the number of contacts quickly rose, it rapidly became infeasible to focus on the activity of just one contact. Instead, the right approach was to use the system to segment on multiple activities and design automated lead nurturing campaigns around those. Hubspot handled all of this effortlessly, but a human has to design the entire approach[35].

This was always something that struck me as odd in my SAP days – SAP just made the assumption that large clients had large, clean, manageable contact databases of millions of people. That was never the case, in reality, and it would be extremely difficult for SAP to match or exceed the capabilities of the Hubspot Platform, though it can be integrated into SAP[36] with a partner solution.

The marketing platform provides the capability to do the marketing. However, it does not replace or even reduce the need for marketers. In fact, it seems to actually require more people, for the simple fact that many marketing channels need their own dedicated resource(s), whether internally, externally or both. We foresee

---

[35] It must be noted that for virtually any system referenced in this book, it still requires a human to set it up. No matter how well designed an automated wizard may be, someone still has to know when, why and how to initiate it.

[36] There are multiple vendors with Hubspot to SAP integrations already. The challenge with integration is knowing what to integrate.

that in the future, much more of the marketing work will be pulled inhouse, almost all overseas work[37] will be brought back and the overall demand for marketers skilled with digital marketing will dramatically increase.

Sales Team

Within the Sales team, you find that they are designing and dealing with automation sequences (workflows), daily reminders, E-Mail templates, messages, chatbots, and meetings. They are also trying to find and use the latest Sales Documents. Sales Management is trying to ensure everybody gets enough leads and the workload is balanced. Then everybody is trying to use lead scoring and now predictive lead scoring.

Hubspot helps Sales Teams with all of these tasks. But the typical sales guy doesn't want to nor have the time to do this on his own. That's why you not only need a super simple CRM like Hubspot, that does most of the data entry work automatically and in the background, you also need Sales Enablement support.

Sequences/Reminders

Like workflows for marketing, sequences are a lite weight tool, thus very simplified, for use by Sales. You can schedule a sequence of sales emails to be sent out, set reminders, create tasks, i.e., like LinkedIn[38] reach out and to do any number of other tasks that you have decided should be part of the sequence.

---

[37]. We have not yet seen any successful overseas marketing providers. The language requirements are too culturally specific. We have seen some success using overseas technical development resources, but they require an extreme amount of overhead to successfully manage.

[38]. We often find clients successfully using Hubspot CRM and LinkedIn Sales Navigator

Templates

Creating Sales E-Mail templates can be both time consuming and yet have a very high ROI. That is why we highly recommend creating and testing templates on an on-going basis. It helps you save time when it comes time to use them, it helps you compare Apples-to-Apples, and it helps you achieve a higher ROI overall on your sales efforts.

The email templates are dynamic, meaning they can use information from your contact and companies database. Given that you may have up to 1,000 fields in your contact database, the creative possibilities are endless. But be advised, simple is usually the most effective. Strangely, text only emails seem to work better than highly stylized image heavy emails.

Messages/Popup Chat

Website chat is one of the most powerful channels you can add to your technology stack. Since it comes built in with all levels of Hubspot, it is a small task to turn it on. That said, someone has to man it, even though it has tactics (Chatbots) for handling those time periods when you're away from the office. But for it to work well, you need to man it, with competent staff.

With the addition of the chatbot functionality, you now need to think through your messaging strategy to make it work.

Meetings/Google Calendar

The integration between Hubspot and Google Calendar has proven to be a real boon to us in our operation, literally keeping my calendar full. Meetings mean sales for our company. Selling highly complex professional services? Just about all sales ultimately involve one or more meetings, and doing it online is cheaper than doing it face-to-face. If you're like me, if it isn't in my calendar, it didn't happen.

Where Should You Use Your Meeting Link

Everywhere. Put it in your email signature and make sure it is also in your mobile phone's e-mail signature. Add it to your lead nurturing email signature. Within Hubspot, you can create a signature that includes your meeting link and store it under your profile. Then it becomes the default for just about everything you send out using the tool.

You can also use it in a Call-To-Action (CTA) within videos you host on youtube. You should also include it on your business card, along with a QR Code. We've even seen it used inside Facebook messenger. In short, you want to make sure everybody in your universe of contacts can easily grab a spot on your calendar.

Even if you don't use Hubspot sales, if you have the minimum paid version of Google GSuite, you can create a meeting link within Google and share it out on all your platforms. Don't know how to do that? There's a course on LinkedIn that will walk you through it step-by-step, but access to the course does require a paid LinkedIn subscription. By the way, the training available on LinkedIN is a great way to spend some training dollars.

Unlimited Sales Document Library

One of the main advantages, if underutilized, capabilities of the Hubspot CRM is the Sales Document Library. It isn't just an online file storage capability. It allows you to conduct one-to-one on-demand webinars using your pre-existing content. It also allows you to measure the performance of not just each document, but each page within a document. This is ideal for enabling marketing to prepare documents for use by sales and to see how they work. It should also allow sales more time to conduct sales versus preparing what could be templated proposals, i.e., templates.

Sales Enablement People

That's people with experience using Hubspot CRM to actually pursue and close deals. The author has used several CRMs over the years, but Hubspot CRM is the only one that actually has helped seal the deal, while the rest were largely after the fact record keeping systems of little value to closing the deal. To help Sales people perform at maximum output, you need to employ four key pieces of the Hubspot CRM:

- Workflows
- Lead Rotators[39]
- Lead Scoring
- Tasks, particularly Call Queues

[39.] I often refer to the President's Club throughout this book and daily speeches. Though it may be called many things, it is always referring to Sales people who have hit quota or overachieved and are now being sent to a company paid sales retreat, typically in a resort location. Top performers get taken care of.

Workflows

Workflows are closely related to sequences in that they automate a series of predefined task. But they allow you to do more than just send out emails in a sequence. For sales, they allow them to process a high volume of leads, sending some back to marketing for further lead nurturing, as one use case.

Lead Rotators/Load Balancing

For any sales team bigger than one person, you need a way to ensure each sales person has a steady flow of leads. That's where the automatic lead rotator comes into play. You can use it to automatically allocate leads to each member of the team. That way, you make sure everybody has an equal amount of work and an equal chance of succeeding against quota. You also can use this functionality to make sure leads, which cost a lot of money to generate, don't fall through the cracks when someone goes on vacation, say, when they go to the annual President's Club get together.

Predictive Lead Scoring

Almost every business owner we've worked with wants to know if the system has lead scoring. Short answer is, yes, it does. The predictive functionality depends on your subscription level. But we have found that most Sales Managers don't quite understand the statistics being used. So we always start by using the manual scoring capability and then as we and it get smarter and the sales volume grows, upgrade to get to the predictive level lead scoring.

Call Queues

A call queue is simply a list of contacts who you need to call. If you're working in an outbound call center, you will need to make a certain number of calls to hit your sales quota. In order to make maximum use of your time, a system will need to line up your calls in what is called a Call Queue. Unless you've seen one, they are hard to visualize, so I am providing an example from within my own Hubspot portal. With this system, as with many others, you click the button to call the lead, and make the sale.

For this to be effective, both from a Sales Closure Rate perspective as well as resource utilization rate, the system needs to provide context to the call center agent. That's why it's so powerful to have an integrated marketing and sales platform. All of the information that has been collected by the marketing system, such as what content they may have consumed, what they have read, previous interactions they may have had with your business, is there for review prior to making the call. Nothing less useful than making a call without any sort of background information.

You may also notice that you have the data to start making sure you have enough leads and call center agents with this type of system. Let's do the math on it real quick. Let's say that for a call to turn into a sale, you've determined that a call that last six minutes usually means a sale was made, while a call that last less than one minute usually means no sale (though that lead may turn into a lead on the next go around). Each hour is sixty minutes long and therefore, the maximum sales per hour for any given sales agent is ten sales per hour. Ten times six minutes is one hour.

Therefore, the maximum potential daily sales for any given sales agent is eight times ten or eighty sales per day. However, no one can work eight hours straight - they need to take breaks and as well, possibly process a sale. I recommend you use a sixty-six percent effective availability for each call center agent. That means you'll get 5.28 hours of available call time from each agent a day. Best case scenario is now about 52 sales a day. However, even the best lead qualification system still does not result in a 100% lead-to-sales conversion rate. It's much more likely to be between ten and fifteen percent. So maybe 5 to 6 sales a day. Some places may make far more sales than this, while others make only one sale a day per agent.

What matters here is that you are generating enough leads to make whatever sales number you have to hit for your business to thrive. Let's do some further, back-of-the-envelope sales math. If your average order value (AOV) is $250.00, then your expected monthly income per sales agent is easily computed as average sales per day times AOV * average workdays per month, which we will assume to be 20. That gives you $250*5*20 or $25,000 per month expected revenue on 5 sales per day. No magic math here, just simple calculations.

Is that enough? Well, there's a few questions to ask to sort of start seeing if your system makes sense. For instance, let's say your Fully Loaded Cost (FLC) of a sales agent is $15 per hour. That's $2,400 a month in salary. You're still good. But how much did the lead cost? There's quite a bit of benchmark data available on cost per lead.

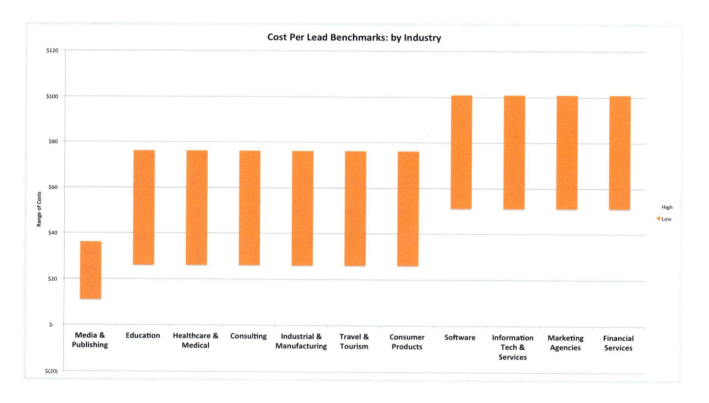

To finish our example, let's use $50 dollars per lead as an average. That's taking into account systems cost, like Hubspot, content production and paid advertising and anything else it takes to get the lead in the door. Roughly speaking, we know we are going to spend $24 dollars of call center agent time to close a deal, so now we have $250-$24=$226 of revenue left to cover the Cost of Lead Generation. If you want to know what the upper limit is on what you can spend to acquire a customer, while still making some profit, you almost have all the information you need. For example, if you would be happy making 35% Gross Profit on a $250 sale, you know you can't spend more than about $163 per sale on lead generation cost. That means if you divide $163/$50, you need to be converting leads-to-customers at about 33% or one out of three.

Why You Want Inbound Leads

It has always been stated that Inbound Leads are about 62% cheaper than outbound lead generation efforts, which includes paid advertising. Inbound Leads also typically convert at a higher rate than do outbound leads. If an Inbound Lead is 62% cheaper to generate than a paid lead, that means your Inbound Lead is costing you $50*.38 or about $31 per lead. That's why you desperately want more Inbound Leads, they're cheaper and result in a higher profit margin.

Solving The IT Explosion AKA The Multi-System Mess

How Many Existing Systems Do You Subscribe To or Have?

Though we just discussed the information explosion with regards to Hubspot, there is a bigger IT Explosion, which we call the Multi-System Mess.

Just about every sales department has multiple IT systems[40]. Take, for example, the client we worked with who was using Salesforce plus Hubspot. They were also using Five9 Call Center software and Zuora, as well as Google Suite. They also used Quickbooks for their financials and had an entire custom built ERP system linking them to their warehouse management system.

Zuora is an enterprise subscription management software[41] which is integrated into Salesforce. Because of the way it works, your product catalog is in Zuora! Because it dealt with the subscriptions, that meant it also needed to talk to Quickbooks.

All of these systems were highly integrated, and each required someone with knowledge about them to manage them. They may just 'plug in' but that never results in a 100% working system. Ever changing business requirements, especially from the sales team, mean that your requirements will change.

Of course, these systems have to be tied into your ERP backbone, or your product won't go out the door. The poor CIO is kept hopping just keeping them all running. But the Sales end user is the one who has to master the software. The Sales Manager, despite having analytics available in Salesforce, always develops spreadsheets to provide him with the information he actually needs. Get it wrong and you mess up commission payments. Now you will truly find out what sales people care about. (Spoiler Alert – Commissions Payments that they agree are correct). Welcome to spreadsheet hell.

---

[40]. Every client has a unique IT System Landscape environment.

[41]. Subscriptions are a way to allow customers to buy the same thing over and over. Think utility bills, newspaper subscriptions, Netflix Subscribers. The subscription economy is huge.

Multiple Systems Lead to Multiple Points of Failure

The more systems you have, whether cloud based or on premise, the more potential failure points you have. Sometimes, these failure points are technical and easily fixed, such as an API key[42] needing to be regenerated and replaced. But more often than not, what this author finds is that there is a difference in data models between the systems, and so the underlying business process functionality doesn't align between the various systems.

Multi-System Mess

While the Sales Team suffers from the multi-system mess caused by employing a multitude of systems, Marketing has its own problems.

Quality Back Links

One of the major factors that determine your website ranking is the number of and quality of the backlinks[43] your website has. Google has gotten much, much better at detecting links which are being generated using link farms.

---

[42] An API key is typically a long string of characters generated by the system which is exchanged with another system. It acts as a lock and opens up a secure communication channel between two or more trusted systems.
[43] A backlink is a hyper link between two different websites.

No More Link Farms or Black Hat

If you are using Hubspot, then you have a good start on fixing it. But many website owners are suffering from past sins, driven in large part by Google's SEO Algorithm getting ever smarter. In the past, many, many companies, both large and small, employed the nefarious services of Black Hat SEO farms[44], usually located in India, the Philippines, Taiwan, China, Pakistan or Sri Lanka. These approaches no longer work as Google grades the quality of your backlinks and will blacklist you if found to be using these techniques.

Now, you have to legitimately earn backlinks by providing a quality user experience. Inhouse Marketing expertise is now necessary and expensive, and getting more so. Any tasks that can be eliminated using marketing automation has to be, just to survive. This also means the budget for marketing has to increase or marketing will not be able to meet its SLA obligations to Sales.

Overseas Website Management No Longer Works

We have come across a large number of customers that were paying for their website to be managed by an overseas, thus low cost, website management service. Unfortunately, we have never found a customer that could actually tell us what these companies were doing for them. Even more surprising is that we have never ran across a business that could say whether they had generated any leads from these services.

---

[44]. Black Hat here refers to using techniques to defeat Google's search algorithm, which Google does not approve of and when detected, can and will result in Google removing the site from the Google search index. This usually results in the 'death' of that website and any business associated with it. Don't use Black Hat.

If this approach ever worked, it no longer does. It was cheap (but no longer is) and as the state of the art has advanced, not really a viable approach. There are services that it makes sense to outsource, say, uploading a parts catalog. Mostly, though, we just have not seen it working as well as having it onshore and inhouse, usually a combination of both.

For some larger corporate customers, they typically are using their website for more than lead generation[45]. They are often times delivering customer support over the web, and there is a never ending quest to drive the cost of that down, even at the expense of good customer service.

High Inhouse Cost Maintenance Manpower Intensive

Hosting and managing a website is also manpower intense and expensive. Few companies go this route. When they do, we usually find that their coding teams create unmanageable platforms that aren't plug'n'play compatible with things like Google Analytics.

Limited Eyeball Time AKA Inventory

You will often hear the term limited inventory. What does that mean, exactly, in the context of digital marketing. Simply put, there's only so much attention available from each user, and places to put ads that make sense for that user at that time with that intent are limited. That's why the auction model used by most

---

[45]. For instance, SAP has a 'behind the firewall' website(s) that provides a multitude of services to customers and implementation partners. No leads are generated from this part of their website. Yet it is critical to the success of the company.

platforms is such a money spinner. Everybody wants and needs to get their message in front of the same audience. The Auction approach ensures both inventory, cost and value are in balance.

Specific Audience

Platforms like Google and Facebook allow you to leverage Artificial Intelligence to target specific audiences based on a variety of factors, such as age, sex, past actions, keyword intent and literally hundreds of others. Each time someone clicks on an ad using Google, Google analyzes approximately 70,000,000 million data points and shows what it believes to be the perfect ad to help the user achieve their goal. Humans have no such capability.

All Require a Perfect Website – Hubpot is a Perfect Website

All of these capabilities and requirements require that you have a perfect website. Hubspot provides you the ability to build and maintain the perfect website. That's why we see the customers with the most success have their entire website 100% hosted on Hubspot. That way, their system is making sure things like links aren't broken, redirects are happening and system reliability is near 100% due to their global delivery network. Without this type of 'system level' capability, your marketing team and sales team would end up spending much of their time fighting technical fires, versus dreaming up better messages, online tools and strategies.

Company Research

If you've worked in sales very long, as this author has, you may remember the days when you had to conduct extensive background research on a client using expensive tools such as Hoovers or Thomas Register. Then along came LinkedIN and social media in general. The integration between Hubspot and LinkedIN has all but eliminated this tedious research. It is done in the background and pulled into the system automatically. You can then be sure you're looking at the right LinkedIN profile when you review it prior to your meeting or call. To put this into perspective – without this capability, this author was lucky to do a deep background check on at most 2 prospects a day. To make it feasible, the number of people who I looked at was intentionally limited. When you have this Hubspot+LinkedIN setup running, you can usually find something on just about everybody in the meeting. For complex sales, such as SAP, it is not unusual to have 5, 10 or 15 people in a meeting and if you walk in cold, building rapport is just not going to happen.

Sequences/Reminders

A sales person is just about always busy, or he better be if he hopes to hit quota. The problem is that today's systems, if not properly setup and managed, can generate a deluge of data which quickly grows out of hand. That's why using sequences and reminders is such a huge advance. Now you can put a prospect in an email sequence, and get reminders that you were supposed to reach out on LinkedIN.

Require Own Strategy/Own Budget/Own Creative/

Because the marketing game is now so much more competitive and dynamic than it was in the past, higher budgets for creative work have to be allocated. In addition, a highly developed content strategy has to be developed and integrated into the marketing platform.

All of this is required to get a company's share of everybody's limited attention span.

All of these items, backlinks, SEO, user tracking, content management, social media publishing, require a perfect website. Hubspot provides a perfect website platform to support both your sales and marketing teams.

Resolving The Human Resource Problem

It can be very hard to scale your marketing efforts if you don't have the right system in place and the right people. When the unemployment rate is very low, it is almost impossible to get highly skilled marketing experts, let alone specialist in each marketing channel. That's why when you get your marketing and sales mix right, where you're getting $2 dollars out for every $1 dollar you put in, you have only one question, how many dollars can you put into your profit-making machine.

The limitation most businesses are facing is that each marketing channel behaves differently, and changes quickly. That's why you need people who can fully exploit each channel, before a competitor shows up and your channel stops working.

You Have to Leverage Every Person's Ability

That means you must equip your marketing team with a system like Hubspot, which is an Inbound Marketing platform. It offers many benefits:

- All-In-One-System
- Mature System/Global System
- Cloud Based SaaS System
- Native Integrations with a wide range of Applications/Software Systems
- Immediate Improvements
- 300+ Engineers to Keep it Running
- Good Responsive Customer Service
- Offers contextual marketing[46] capabilities

You may ask yourself, why don't I just piece together a system from something like WordPress, and use Google Analytics. You could, but what you will quickly find out is the tracking systems are both imperfect and undergoing constant development. No matter how much money and time you invest in setting up your various Google tracking codes, there will never be a time when you aren't tinkering with the Google Analytics tracking code or Facebook Pixel or any of the other tracking codes you have to insert.

On the other hand, Hubspot's tracking code is designed to work with a fully hosted Hubspot platform, and tells you what you need to know as a marketer. Google and most other tracking code providers are increasingly

---

46.   Contextual marketing is a capability of a website to modify the information a user sees based on past user behavior.

providing you with less useful information[47], which ultimately means that your marketing expenses are going to go up. When you have the information available to you that Hubspot generates[48], it means your marketing team can concentrate on using the information provided to do better marketing, at scale, rather than trying to fix broken tracking codes.

Interactive Tool Development Platform

Marketing people have a complex job these days, and development, in the sense of interactive tools, is an increasingly important part of the marketing mix. Hubspot allows you to develop highly interactive online tools, and track how well they work. All within the tool. There are other platforms that allow marketers to dream up and build interactive tools as well, which are integrated into Hubspot.

Use Tools to Leverage Precious Human Resources

This is how you leverage your human resources – using systems that automate much of the work, while allowing marketers to get ever more creative. In 2008, it was state-of-the-art to put a whitepaper or eBook behind a form to collect an email and start to move someone through a planned sequence of events. Today, in 2018, that is table stakes. You still have to do those.

---

[47]. Google search terms have been encrypted by Google for at least five years. That means Google never tells you what term a user used to find your website. Other websites, such as DukDuk Go, base their entire business model on anonymous searches.

[48]. Hubspot shows who converted on what page. With the Google Search Console integration, you know what search term a user used on Google.com when Google decided to show your page.

But to win against your competitors, you have to provide interactive content. This can take many forms, from value calculators, to product selectors and quizzes to interactive video. With the available tools, a marketer can create any of these types of tools without a coder. The challenge then becomes for the marketer to uncover the type of tool someone might find useful. We have a process we follow to do this for our own tools, which we develop inhouse.

It isn't all that complicated. For example, for calculators, the first step is to build it in excel. Can you break it there? Then it is not ready yet to be converted into an online tool. We have often times created an excel based calculator template, and once we saw that a lot of people were downloading it, we converted it into an online tool. That way, we can upgrade the functionality and create a lead generation tool, also known as a lead magnet. For instance, our online, interactive SAP BW Project Estimator was developed from a very complex tool which, frankly speaking, we had trouble using on actual projects. But it was constantly being downloaded. That meant we weren't gaining any useful knowledge from actual estimates.

So, given that our team is composed of Business Intelligence experts, this author included, we spent about a week seeing if there wasn't a way to simplify the estimate so you didn't depend on having SAP knowledge at all. What we came up with uses only the information a business user would have, adds in some 'planning friction' and then produces both an estimate and an interactive map that breaks it down for you. It takes less than a minute for what used to take several weeks by some of the world's top minds.

We then ran estimates against a large number of projects we had already worked on to ensure the estimates are valid. They were 'close enough' for government work, often times being precisely right.

Now that tool is used by a huge number of clients who are getting ready to start an SAP BW project. We just happen to get insight into how many SAP BW consultants they will be needing to do their project, every time they run the project estimator, which is what our business was founded to sell. By the way, that model, of delivering a piece of valuable content, in return for a qualified lead, is one you can and should use in your own business.

We have found similar calculations buried within all kinds of industries, and the process of producing it in excel first, then making sure it won't break and seems to be useful, always works. One of our most unusual calculators was designed to help someone who is preparing a construction bid determine cost differentials between various cities. The client had actual cost data available, so it was just a matter of finding the conversion formula and using the database to create an online tool that has been used by construction contracts worth many billions of dollars.

Over 300 Engineers Working On Hubspot

Hubspot never stops rolling out new capabilities, including Artificial Intelligence (AI) based systems, such as chatbots, integrated video and about 25 other new 'experiments' a month. In fact, with a reported 300 software engineers working on the system, this is one of the key benefits of having the system. You get a lot of engineering work done for you, on an ongoing basis, which is valuable. What are they working on? For one, they work with a large number of software providers to ensure the integration works between Hubspot and their systems.

They are also constantly working on making the system more stable, and faster[49]. In the world of Google, faster response times are a major determinant of whether a user will accomplish their goal.

That's why you need to hire good help and equip them with the absolute best systems available. But beyond that, you need to make sure the people you hire are constantly learning and trying new things.

Solving The No Budget Problem

How's Your Budget?

Without an Adequate Budget You Can't Try a New System to Solve[50] This Problem

Do you have one? All of these Sales and Marketing system requirements require adequate, and most likely, substantial budget, to meet. There's nothing more wasteful or frustrating to have your marketing guy define system requirements, find solutions, and then ask for budget, only to be told no, there is no budget for it. If there is no budget, why did you want someone to look at the problem in the first place?

---

[49]   For instance, the Hubspot blog is already Google AMP enabled. AMP is the Google standard for mobile pages and stands for Accelerated Mobile Pages.

[50]   Transparent pricing is a differentiating factor for most websites.

Numerous Systems and Services Exist That Would Make Sense but the Budget is not There

So how do you work through the budget problem. It all goes back to setting that top line revenue goal or quantified vision. Most software companies, including Hubspot, have their pricing right on their website. But your budget is going to consist of much more than your Hubspot software subscription. It will consist of:

- Marketing Expertise
- Creative Design and Production
- Paid Advertising, i.e., PPC
- Events
- Development Support
- Training

Lack of Understanding True Value of a Lead

There are many more items that must be budgeted for. That's why you need to know the true value of a lead. Otherwise, all budget talk will be about how little you can spend, versus how much value you can capture. Ask most business owners, even large businesses, what the value of a lead is and they will say nothing. It has no value until it converts into a customer. That's why it's handy to know how to compute the value of a lead. In his book, "The Acceleration Formula", Mark Roberge, an MIT trained engineer, explains how he was able to develop a picture of his buyers based on where they are at in each stage of the marketing funnel.

Using some simple math, based on the probability of closing into a sale, he was able to show what each lead was worth at each stage of their sales funnel. There are also courses available on LinkedIN that go over this same concept. Still, how do you know a lead has any value or rather potential value? First, you spent money to generate those leads. So that's the cost perspective. Secondly, if you know your conversion rates, meaning you have an idea about your conversion rate at each stage of your sales funnel, you know how often your marketing system succeeded in converting a contact into a customer. As Peter Drucker said, the sole purpose of a business is to create a customer.

Using Lead Value to Put Marketing On a Revenue Budget

Once you know how to define what each lead is worth to you, when you add them up, you have a good idea of how much revenue you're going to produce. Starts to sound a whole lot like an extended Sales Forecast when you take this approach. If you intend to generate $1,000,000 a year in revenue, and you know that your Marketing and Sales funnel has 3 stages in it that convert at 10%, you know how many website visitors you have to generate to hit that number. If you hit your website visitor number and leads generated number but not your sales made number, you know you have a sales problem, either sales person related or offer related.

Budget Based on Target Revenue

It should be obvious that it requires a large marketing budget to achieve your revenue goals. With this approach of putting marketing on a revenue goal, and you developing a revenue target, now you can decide how much you should spend on the marketing side of the house. With literally 6,000 plus marketing systems (and rising) available, which is an explosion in systems since 2008, it is very easy to get carried away or to just freeze up and make no decision. As Napoleon Hill, author of "Think & Grow Rich" said, to succeed, you must have a desire to make a definite amount of money. Sounds a lot like have a quantified vision to this author.

CHAPTER FOUR

PRICING HUBSPOT AND OTHER SYSTEMS

How to Size and Price the Hubspot System

Sizing the Hubspot System

Like all software systems, in order to acquire Hubspot, you first have to size it. Though their pricing changes from time to time, the basics of sizing it don't. Hubspot is sold on an annual subscription basis, whose base price is composed of a subscription plus a fee based on the number of contacts you have in your system. Beyond these two primary sizing components, there are a number of other add-ons, such as transactional email IPs, Reports Add-On and other items which need to be considered.

We've actually designed an online tool for people to use to determine their requirements. There are also free versions of their marketing and sales tools which are ideal for small businesses who are just starting out. Be warned, however, that you cannot do full Inbound Marketing without at least the professional level of the tool. By the time this book comes out, they may well have dropped their entry level subscription, for the simple fact that it is doesn't allow you to do all you need to do when it comes to Inbound Marketing.

Our recommendation is always to start with at least the professional level subscription and to host your entire website on the Hubspot platform. The only thing they do not provide is your domain. We recognize that some companies have complex website structures which it may not be possible to migrate fully to Hubspot. For the most part, those websites don't generate leads and are for other purposes. What are the major functionalities or cost you are absorbing if you're not 100% hosting your website on Hubspot:?

- You **severely limit** what you can do with contextual marketing
- You lose a tremendous amount of expensive marketer **productivity** when they aren't operating 100% within the Hubspot platform
- You really can't do **A/B testing** easily, if at all.
- You **don't have the complete visibility** into each contact's activity.
- You **can't do campaign analytics** without having it all in Hubspot

Let's breakdown what each of the above actually means.

You severely limit what you can do with contextual marketing. First off, you need to understand what we mean by contextual marketing when using Hubspot. If you've ever noticed an email comes to you with your first name in it, you have an inkling of what you can do with contextual marketing, but that is only scratching the surface. The much bigger deal with contextual marketing is that you make the page a user sees dynamically change its content based on a huge number of factors the system knows about the user. The more often the user engages with the website, the more contextually relevant the content can be for each user. That's why it is important to have all your content hosted within Hubspot – it really can't completely change the content on a WordPress site for you.

You lose a tremendous amount of expensive marketer productivity when they aren't operating 100% within the Hubspot platform. Though the platform's strength is its ease of use, it still takes some time to master it. Once mastered though, a Hubspot user can design, develop and deploy a new offering in a few minutes. When measured against advanced users of platforms like WordPress, the productivity level differences are stark. This author has set up Thank You Pages, Landing Pages, Forms, Smart Lists, Work Flows, Email Lead Nurturing Sequences, Blog Posts and Paid Campaigns, all in under an hour, that a highly experienced WordPress consultant took 3 days to do.

It took a long time to reach that level of productivity. Here's the thing. The speed of the tool isn't the important thing to keep in mind here. What's important is that instead of worrying about how to set up all those complex bits-n-pieces of a campaign, an Inbound Marketer can spend the time thinking about the actual content, the key words, the copywriting, in short, the creative part.

This productivity impact also relates to the contextual marketing issue previously discussed. Setting up contextual marketing represents a whole other level of expertise. You need to have mastered a tool that makes it simple to do, because thinking through what you want a particular visitor to 'experience' based on what can be complex parameters, is a mind bender. It's interesting to do, but it not something a casual user is going to do well.

A/B testing is one of the key tools in a marketer's sandbox as is multivariate testing. Don't confuse this with contextual marketing. In this case, we're running 2 different versions of something and evaluating the results with statistics to pick a winner. It is also entirely possible that we are incorporating contextual marketing within an A/B test page. At this level of operations, you're looking for marketers who understand some basic statistics who can also dream up variations and make honest evaluations of the results.

Knowing what a contact has done since the beginning of time on your website is important, but it can represent an overwhelming amount of information. We've worked with sites that get only a few 'conversions' each month, and for these guys, there is time and value at looking at the complete activity record of each contact. We've also worked with website's that are generating thousands to hundreds of thousands of website visits per day. At this level of contact activity, you will never have the time to focus on a single contact's activity. Instead, you will want to look at group behaviors. For instance, people who looked at your pricing page, then did something else. If these same websites also use a lot of lot of third party integrated tools, like webinars, then you will want to see that contact activity as well. It can get really complicated to make sense of this volume of information, let alone formulate a response.

Campaign analytics are also critical to understanding how you're doing. They allow you to evaluate the totality of your offer. Any part of your offer that is not 'inside' the Hubspot platform won't form a part of your campaign analytics and thus, will impede an analyst's ability to draw the right conclusion.

There are many other good reasons to go 100% to a Hubspot hosted solutions, but these are the ones we find are the 'killer apps' you need to know about. It's already a huge challenge to get it right and make full use of the Inbound Marketing methodology when you're on Hubspot, so why complicate your life by keeping your money machine in a mixed, non-productive environment?

Enterprise vs Professional Level of Hubspot

The difference between Enterprise and Professional level Hubspot is substantial, but for many small to mid-size companies, professional will be where they start. Since contact charges are the major difference in the two subscription packages, you should know that the magic number is around 38,000 contacts. This is the point where the math works out to go ahead and switch to the enterprise version of the software.

Because it is cloud based, you really never exceed its transaction processing capability, at least up to 27,000 contacts per day, which was the peak we've experienced with a client. However, if you're using it in a retail environment, meaning e-commerce, and are moving a lot of orders, you will want several add-ons, such as the transactional email with dedicated IP. Transactional emails are things like shipping notifications. Transactional emails are normally treated differently by SPAM filters. These types of emails are meant to keep customers informed about their transaction and thus, not normally a marketing channel - but just keeping customers happy is still a form of marketing.

For smaller operations, a good place to start is with Hubspot Basic, which starts at around $50 a month and provides you the ability to generate conversions using a Hubspot form and to send out one-off marketing emails.

For all others, the FREE version is the way to go. Their CRM FREE system allows you to store up to one million contacts and this usually exceeds the need of most businesses we have run across. Its most important benefit is that is provides a place for you to actually store and organize your contact information.

Add-Ons

There are also a number of add-ons, all of which should be considered when sizing and budgeting for your new system. Website hosting is an add-on (as of the writing of this book) and as we have previously stated, we always recommend moving your complete website to Hubspot's hosting service.

If you do not do this, you're not going to get the full benefit of the automation platform. There are also some key functionalities that cannot function in a mixed environment, at least not easily. Among these is the contextual marketing capability, which is the ability to change the content a user sees based on what the system knows about the user. This can be anything from knowing what content download they downloaded in the past, to what pages they have previously visited, to what marketing channel they are coming to you from and how they got there, for example, a Google PPC advertising campaign.

There are times when a migration isn't technically possible but it is almost always due to the site being used to deliver customer support. However, with the release of the Hubspot service marketplace component, which provides the ability to track customer support tickets, provides a knowledge base capability and allows you to route service requests" to the field support engineering team, this has now largely been eliminated as a reason not to migrate 100% of your website to the Hubspot platform.

The Reporting Add-On is also extremely useful, even with the extensive analytics built into the system. It has helped answer many customer questions that otherwise would have required a Spreadsheet exercise.

The Sales Hub

The Sales tool is priced[51] based on users and starts at $400 a month for 5 users and 80$ a month for each additional user above that number.[52] It also has various add-ons, including the reporting add-on previously mentioned and an API add-on, which is going to be needed if you do a large volume of sales with Salesforce and other tools.

CRM

Although somewhat confusing, CRM is actually a separate tool from the Sales tool and is free. It provides a number of functionalities that most sales people will find invaluable, such as notifying you when someone has opened your email, and the ability to call a prospect directly from within a contact record while on your mobile phone.

Evaluation to See If You Are a Good Fit For Hubspot

Though it may seem like we are proposing Inbound Marketing using the Hubspot platform as the solution to every business' marketing needs, that's not the case. Here's the lowdown. If your product or service isn't

---

[51.] Hubspot pricing is subject to change and the final pricing is always determined at the time of purchase.

[52.] https://www.Hubspot.com/pricing/marketing

worth at least $500 and if you're product or service isn't what is known as a considered sale, then it isn't really a good fit for you. But, if you don't meet this basic criteria, the free version of the tool is almost always of some value to your business.

Is Your Product or Service a Good Fit Inbound?

Do You Know What's a Considered Sale?

This is the odd sounding name for a product or service that requires research by consumers prior to making a purchase decision, be they end consumers or business consumers. Let's break that down. Pre-Internet, it was very difficult for a consumer to conduct research on their own on a vast range of products. That meant they were often dependent on a salesmen to tell them what they needed to know. For small purchases, say, a pair of pants, they just saw and bought it. For larger products, say, a couch, they might drive around to a few stores and compare various options and choose one. They might even have seen someone in their family purchase a model they liked and that became social proof.

For business buyers, there was a vast array of information resources, usually catalogs, and salesmen. There was also a fairly limited selection of products. That has changed. Dramatically so. According to Brian Halligan, there are now approximately five times as many suppliers for every product and service out there, all fighting for the deal. It's great for buyers, but overwhelming.

What it all boils down to is that customers have to do their research before making a purchase decision. You need a system to make sure they are able to evaluate your offer easily and online.

Going Deeper On The Concept of a Considered Sale

This term was new to us when we first heard it, so don't feel bad if you don't know what it means. A product or service falls into the 'considered sale' category if a potential customer has to perform product research before buying it. Though almost every product a consumer purchases requires some level of decision making, say, buying a can of beans, it usually makes little financial sense, from a marketing perspective, to attempt to influence such purchases using the Inbound Marketing methodology. However, even the most mundane products can experience a positive uplift in sales, if the right kind of content can be produced and distributed to the right audience at the right price.

For instance, one of our clients, who also happens to run a promotional marketing agency, ran a contest to find the best rice recipe from among consumers in Southern Spain. Over 14,000 rice recipes were entered in the contest, and these recipes were subsequently used to promote additional purchases of rice.

A more typical 'considered sale' might be for services, such as, in our own business' case, SAP Consulting services. Our core business is selling the expertise of our consultants, which is a very high value service, often costing well over $200 an hour, and sometimes as much as $600 for 'super specialist'. Here, content in the form of Thought Leadership can and has worked very well.

Products costing more than five hundred dollars usually also fall into the considered sale category. Why five hundred dollars? Because of the cost involved in generating the lead for such products. The same holds true for services. That's why it is critical to know what you're selling and for how much.

Are You Ready For Hubspot

Another major consideration when deciding if Hubspot is a good fit for you is whether you have an internal marketing department. Smaller firms, meaning firms with less than $1,000,000 in an annual sales, typically do not have a dedicated marketing person. Once you get to $3 to 5 million in annual revenue, you start to see firms have dedicated marketing staffs. In addition, the firm needs to either be in high-growth mode or in a rapidly changing market.

Channel Sales

This is also typically not a good fit for Hubspot. The brand is usually responsible for doing the channel marketing and in many cases, the product is commoditized, even if orders may be very large, like well casing or coal. It doesn't mean buyers aren't looking for information when they buy, it is just that they often are small contractors and can't spend a lot of time making decisions about which duct tape, tube, or wire to buy.

Does Your Business Know What a Contact, Lead or Prospect Is?

The more your company has a clear idea of what each of these is, the better fit Hubspot will be for them. Though there is no hard and fast, universally accepted rule on what each of these terms means, within the marketing world, most people have a clear idea. For small business owners without much marketing experience, direct marketers, and retailers all have a hard time differentiating between these terms.

Do You Have an Established Sales Process?

This may sound obvious, but in reality, even the largest companies struggle with this one. For a smaller firm, initially, their sales process is thought to be a straight forward case of we find someone (or they find us), and if we have what they want, they buy from us. If only it were that simple.

Multiple Sales Approaches for Multiple Buying Approaches

Most companies are trying to 'professionalize' their buying process. For the seller, this translates into RFPs (Request for Proposals), and other administrative devices, designed explicitly to make the purchase decision be about the lowest possible cost. Of most significance to the seller, it is designed to defeat your attempt to sell on value.

For the seller, Hubspot represents a potential silver bullet. You see, corporate buyers are not walking around their company's floor looking for things to buy, like new software systems. These business requirements are boiling up from within the corporation, sometimes from the CIO (for IT systems and Services) and a lot of times from the CMO, for marketing systems[53], which, by definition, are also IT systems. Sometimes, engineering is buying completely new production processes laden with IT capabilities, while other times, the CEO is driving it. Purchasing is there to try to get the best deal, for them, not the seller.

Hubspot allows all of these buyers to conduct their own research, which for the seller is a good thing.

[53.] Marketing and Sales systems now represent a larger expenditure than all other IT systems combined in most companies.

Do You Have an E-Commerce Store?

If you have an online e-commerce store, Hubspot can be an incredibly valuable addition to your technology stack. Again, you have to do your numbers here, as the margins in e-commerce are often thin. But a platform like Shopify[54], which Hubspot is now natively integrated to, doesn't provide much in the way of content marketing or even email marketing, which is what Hubspot brings to the e-commerce game. Within the Shopify world, there are 100s of partner apps to fill the gap[55], but Hubspot is the premier platform for bringing content marketing to bear on e-commerce.

Online Social Presences

Medium/Linkedin/Google/Amazon/Shopify/Facebook/Instagram/Pinterest/Blog/Twitter/Xing

If you're not present on any of these channels already, then Hubspot probably isn't going to be much of a boost to you. But if you do use any of these channels, want to get more value out of them, and meet all the other 'good fit' criteria, then Hubspot can really boost your results on each of these channels.

For maximum success with each of these channels, you have to develop the right social media strategy. Not all channels are a good fit for all products and services, though there is a surprisingly large amount of overlap.

[54.] Shopify is a cloud based ecommerce platform with a reported one million plus stores running on it.

[55.] We usually find that our e-commerce customers, who are on Shopify, will end up running between 20 and 30 apps within their Shopify Store. The reason being that they need systems to cover all the rest of the business areas, such as Logistics and Finance, plus many apps are useful add-ons to the store itself.

How's Your Budget?

We already talked about how Hubspot is priced. Since it changes from time-to-time, we believe you must also have a clear idea of what you should be spending on marketing. The simplest metric is a percentage of top-line revenue. For instance, L'Oreal, a large, very old, well established firm, recently reported their marketing spend at 30% of revenue in their annual report – even going so far as to break it out on a separate line item.

Here's how to get to the macro level number. Let's say your annual revenue goal is $1,000,000, which is about $83,333 a month in revenue. If you believe 20% is a reasonable marketing spend, then your first pass number is a pretty simple $16,666 a month.

If your product meets the minimum value for Hubspot to be a good fit, then $500 per sale[56] is a number you can do your planning with (it actually forms the lower boundary of an optimization curve you could plot).

At $500 per sale, to hit $83,333 a month in revenue, you need 166 customers a month. So let's say you have a nice even 10% conversion rate from visits to leads to Customers (which eliminates 2 layers of the typical sales funnel). That would mean for every 100 site visitors, you get 10 leads into your system, and for every 10 leads, you generate one customer. To get 166 customers, you then need 1,660 leads and 16,600 site visitors.

Using the value of a lead calculator available on our website, you find that each lead in your system is worth $50. In other words, you could spend some number less than but up to $50 per lead on marketing and still

---

[56.] You can also use the Total Lifetime Value as a benchmark, but we have found that the closer the TLV is to $500, the less likely the math works.

make money. So, if you're spending $16,666 a month on marketing, and you're generating 16,600 visitors, then you're spending about $1 per site visitor, or $10 per lead or 100 dollars per sale.

Given these rough figures, you can see the cost of Hubspot, at the professional level, is going to run a minimum of $1,100 a month or $16,200 a year. That doesn't leave much for paid advertising or marketing talent.

At that rate of contact accumulation, in month 3 you will be at the enterprise level due to passing the 38,000 contacts threshold, which is approximately where it makes sense to go onto the enterprise level versus the professional level.

Once you run these numbers, realize that the typical marketing agency has to charge at least $150 an hour for Inbound Marketing Consulting, and that Paid Advertising will typically make up a large proportion of your marketing spend, at least in the early stages, you begin to see that 20% marketing spend may not be realistic.

However, if you run these numbers for a $5,000,000 a year run rate, you see that it is very doable. Let's try those numbers out for comparison.

Now you need to generate 833 sales a month. Your conversion rate remains the same. To get 833 sales a month, you need 8,330 new contacts each month, and you need 83,300 unique site visits each month. If you're still spending 20% of revenue on marketing, you're spending about $83,300 a month on marketing. Your Hubspot trial subscription cost will be about the same but will rise to the enterprise level in the first month. So we will assume it will be enterprise since day one, since by the end of the year, you would be at

100k contacts. Your monthly Hubspot bill will be $3,600 a month. Let's round that up to $4000 a month so you can get all the add-ons and not have to be wishing you had the reporting, hosting, API calls etc., you really need. That leaves $79,300 to spend from your marketing budget. Let's say you contract an Inbound Marketing Agency, like SAP BW Consulting, Inc. to do all your marketing and they charge $15,000 a month. That leaves $64,300 to spend on content creation and paid media.

All of this means you're spending the same $1 per site visitor, the same $10 dollars per lead and the same $100 dollar per sale.

The picture changes in year two of your Hubspot investment. A major portion of your investment in year one can and must be on content creation. It is a question of both quantity and quality. We can't give you a formula for how much you will need to spend on each piece of content, though we have built a calculator that will give you a rough idea of how much content you're going to need (almost everything you do with content marketing can, in fact, be estimated). There are some content creation platforms where you can get an idea of costs on things such as White Papers, Checklist and Expert Guides. But the creation of content is only one part of the content creation puzzle, the other is blogging and promotion. The fundamental Inbound Content model involves a piece of content, usually behind a form, and a Blog with a Call-to-Action (CTA) in it. Blogs can cost as little as $350 to write but more typically, we are seeing it be closer to $500 (and up and rising rapidly) for a well-researched, SEO optimized blog. Once written, the blog just keeps on working, day-in, day-out. Paid advertising[57], on the other hand, is rented attention. It is 'use once', pay again to use it again. But you will need to spend heavily on it, because the competition for all forms of attention is intense and growing.

[57.] Paid Advertising is used by more than 50% of all Inbound Marketers. It's also the route to scaleability.

We work closely with each of our clients to set realistic expectations around expected results and cost. It all comes down to having a working sales funnel as to which approach makes sense.

Sales

Though Sales and CRM[58] are technically 2 different pieces of software in Hubspot world, we're going to treat them as a single whole. That's because they work better together than apart.

The Hubspot CRM/Sales Software is priced according to seats, and allows you to store up to 1 million contacts in the free version, which is a lot of contacts. As you add contacts, there is a scalable fee which varies by the number of contacts you're keeping. There are currently 4 versions or subscription levels, Free, Starter, Professional and Enterprise.

The system was originally rolled out as a highly simplified, limited functionality CRM system, which was designed to solve one single problem above all others – make it easy and painless for salespeople to enter data in the system. As it has evolved, it has kept this core functionality, while adding many additional capabilities, like the ability to generate a quote and close a deal, right from within the system.

---

58.   CRM, or Customer Relationship Management, is defined differently by different vendors.

How Do You Dominate a Market?

Dominating a market really comes down to having a working sales process that yields enough profit for you to outspend any competitor on marketing. Let me repeat that – if you have a working sales funnel and it generates enough profit for you to outspend your competitors, you can take 80% of the market, while leaving the 20% to your competitors. Perry Marshall, of 80/20 fame, even provides a handy online calculator that allows you to demonstrate this for yourself.

Google will also help out you here. Within Google Adwords, they publish a nice little chart for your campaigns that tells you how much of the available first page/first position ad space you are capturing with your adwords campaign. If you're making enough money to outbid your competitors to capture the lion's share of the 1st place position, then you will garner virtually all the clicks. But what if you don't yet have either enough money to buy the top position or a proven sales funnel to do this. You need an Inbound Marketing platform.

Because Hubspot is an integrated Inbound Marketing and Sales platform, you have an ideal tool with which to generate leads and pursue and close sales, using both paid and organic, as well as social, email and direct campaigns. It was very common before the CRM was released for deals to get lost in the marketing system. Sure, you could bolt Salesforce onto it, and many have and do, including Hubspot itself. But Salesforce is costly, and relies on a datamodel that is fundamentally different from Hubspot.

Within the professional services space, such as SAP consulting, this tool really shines. It can easily track deals, either from within your office or while on the road using the mobile app version of it. It allows you to call and track clients, all right within the tool. Though it is not an Inbound Call center application, there are integrated partner products already available that turn it into one. This places it firmly in competition with Salesforce and Call Center Telephony software, like Five9™ Call Center software, as well as many others.

It is, however, an outbound call center capable application. You can use the integrated VOIP calling capability of the CRM to make outbound calls. You can call from within your browser or telephone. You can then create and manage call scripts for use by your sales team. You also will automatically have a record of the calls you made to each individual contact. You can record them as well. Of course, you can report on a large number of call characteristics, such as number of call attempts and connects.

Make Marketing Provide Materials to Sales

Because you can store marketing materials right within it, the marketing team can easily track what is being used, what is helping, what is not and they can figure out how to support the sales team.

Sales People Need Automation Tools

With Hubspot's sequence tool, sales people can drop leads into what are called automated workflows known as sequences so they never At high volumes, this becomes critical as it is very easy to lose track of valuable contacts. You would be amazed at how much value is lost by large companies because their sales team simply loses track of deals and the people they are working with within the accounts.

It also benefits highly from its tight integration with LinkedIN Sales Navigator and Pandadoc. One allows your sales team to easily pull in information about contacts while the other allows you to generate beautiful, interactive proposals, and tie them back to the contacts. Keeping track of who you have sent what contract proposal to can quickly get complicated when you have hundreds or even thousands of them out on the street at any given time.

It is also possible to integrate the tool either natively or via Zapier to your accounting system, which allows you to create accurate account records, including invoices and projects, on the fly. For complex services, with multi-level BOM[59]s, this is a critical issue. It is not yet at the level of SAP, but since it will integrate to SAP, I foresee this capability coming soon.

Marketing

Hubspot is an Inbound Marketing platform. In fact, the founders are credited with developing the term 'Inbound Marketing'. In the ideal setup, a company's website is completely hosted on Hubspot's SaaS platform[60]. It is designed to allow marketers to make almost any kind of change to the system without relying on developers. It does, however, provide an extensive development capability for those cases where you want to create things like online product selectors and calculators.

At its core, it allows a piece of content to be 'gated' behind a form, and for you to generate blogs and to use CTAs to generate interest and drive people to becoming a contact in your system.

[59.] BOM or Bill of Materials. Usually a list of materials required to make a product arranged in some sort of hierarchical order. You can also have Service BOMS. As well, there are various types of BOMs, depending upon the business requirement.

[60.] SaaS, Software as a Service

It is also a sophisticated SEO or Search Engine Optimization machine, with SEO optimization tools available at every level of the system. It automatically takes care of technical issues, like sitemaps, redirects, and SSL so a marketer can concentrate on developing and delivering content.

The Subscription Sizes

There are, at the time of this writing, three paid versions of Hubspot and one Free version. Because the offering changes from time to time, I am going to discuss the highlights and provide some guidance on which system is probably the best fit for you.

Free

There are free versions of both the marketing and sales platforms. These are great solutions for small businesses who are just getting started. They are really there to help Hubspot penetrate the Wordpress market of 125 million sites.

That said, you can capture leads from a Wordpress site with the system and many other types of sites, just depending on how they built their forms. With the Hubspot tracking code installed, you can also get a lot of useful information about who has visited your site, something which Google makes increasingly difficult.

The CRM tool is an excellent tool for storing contacts, and we highly recommend it for any business. Almost every small business has a mess of a contact management system, and this simple tool is typically a quantum leap in efficiency for them.

Basic

The basic level allows you to do some of what is considered Inbound Marketing (at least as far as how Hubspot defines it), but we usually do not recommend it as it doesn't allow you to do much of the automated lead nurturing.

It is, however, a good place to start if you have a limited website with little content. You can still couple it with an Inbound Marketing Content Strategy development effort to start getting organized.

Professional

We nearly always recommend our clients start with the professional level and have their entire website hosted on Hubspot. Why? Because it is only at this level that you can do two critical tasks:

- Set up automated lead nurturing email sequences driven by Smart Lists and workflows
- Supercharge your website with contextual marketing.

What is Contextual Marketing?

If you ever seen a website show you content specific to you, then you have an idea about contextual marketing. With Hubspot, the more it knows about a visitor, the more it can adjust what it shows to that visitor so that it meets their exact requirements.

To do this, everything needs to be on Hubspot. If you mix and match delivery platforms, it just won't work.

This is not to say that it magically adjust content. No indeed. It takes a human being with deep understanding of your particular buyer personas, the ability to plan in advance how the system should adjust the content to the user's needs and to be able to measure and adjust the content strategy based on results. In other words, you have to methodically plan out the response to everything. The last thing a marketing team needs to be spending time on is trying to do this across multiple platforms.

The ability to adjust what a user sees can be driven by any number of characteristics, such as search term used, membership on a list, number of pages visited, email response, amount spent, video viewed, and many others.

It is also at this level you can use Smart Forms, which adjust which fields are shown based on what has already been provided by a user. This is especially valuable when you know a user has to visit your site many times before they make it all the way through your marketing and sales funnel. You can progressively profile a lead and find out pretty much anything, if you ask for the information in tiny chunks. But don't be asking for information that will never be used by either marketing or sales. It reduces conversion rates and drives users crazy. Hubspot can be set to never ask for existing information it has about someone, or can ask for all it every time or just some of it. You can and should experiment with this.

This subscription level is also the minimum level where you can start to set up behavior-based email flows. This is slightly different from just sending out a series of pre-planned emails in response to one event. This is the ability to send them down different forks in the road based on combinations of other activities.

Enterprise

The enterprise level of Hubspot is truly where the big boys play. In addition to all of the functionality of professional, it provides a number of advanced features that are especially needed for very high volume enterprises.

Event Based Responses

This is the ability to respond with an email or phone call based on knowing that someone just looked at your pricing page. You can also make your website pop up chat[61] only pop up in response to such an event.

Custom Event Reporting

This is closely related to being able to respond to events. Because you can set up an almost infinite number of events, you need a way to report on them.

This is closely associated with event based responses.

---

61. Pop up chat refers to the little chat windows you see on many websites that, if you click on them, connects you directly with a human being.

Predictive Lead Scoring

This one is always critical to Sales. If there is sufficient lead volume, then you want the ability to have the system send you only the leads with the highest probability to close. Predictive Lead Scoring is how you do that.

Content Partitioning

This is a fancy way of saying you can segregate content by marketing teams. This is critical for multi-national teams where content is created in multiple languages.

Single Sign-On

Within most enterprises, there is a requirement for SSO or Single Sign On. This means that any system within the enterprise has to share security information with a central security management system (think LDAP[62] or Light Weight Directory Access Protocol) such that when a user signs onto one system, they get access to all the systems they are authorized to use and need to use to accomplish their jobs. This is a tremendous time saver – when it works right, which can be tricky to pull off.

[62.] Although controlling which users have access to which content is necessary, you would be well advised to make sure your users truly have all the access they need, not just what some IT Security Guy may have arbitrarily decided long ago.

Can You Afford This System?

Can You Afford NOT to Get This Systems?

These are two key questions you must ask and get answers to. As you can see from our previous chapter on the cost of the system, you can do some fine-grained figuring as far as cost. That's the thing about digital marketing, it means you can measure a lot that was never measurable before.

Unfortunately, it is not a write a check and get your marketing and sales problem solved. If it was, there would be no end of people just writing checks and expecting more money to come back. This system requires a business owner, in the case of small enterprises to the marketing department in large enterprises, to take on a lot of new responsibilities.

When we started out, we had to learn this from the ground up, which means we've already walked up a complex, steep learning curve. The author was already a highly successful quota carrying Industry Principal for a major ERP vendor, SAP.

Why We Decided on the Inbound Marketing Approach to Business

Each year while working for SAP, the author had to submit an annual business plan. So, starting from the quota and working backwards, an exhaustive amount of planning was done across all activities required to hit quota. This included developing a detailed marketing plan, among many other activities. Each year,

SAP recommended[63] we do more Inbound Marketing but couldn't really explain what it was. So they had Hubspot do a demonstration one day, and now, even SAP is a Hubspot customer. We've now been doing this for almost 10 years, for a variety of clients, including ourselves, across a broad swath of industries, including e-commerce, TV, Professional Services, Insurance and Retailers. We know it works.

When we started our own Inbound Marketing journey, there were no Inbound Marketing partners, or we would have written a check to have one take this on. Now, almost 400 content pieces later, and more than 400 blogs later, and achieving Hubspot Gold Tier partner level, we know our clients need this solution. That effort has yielded a huge number of leads, customers and prospects from within the SAP space as well as from the broader Hubspot market space. In fact, we are a primary content reference source for SAP employees themselves!

Paid Consulting/Coaching/8 Years Successful Experience with Hubspot and Inbound Marketing & Social Media

We also know that our customers need help with implementing it, and that's why we offer paid consulting for both Inbound Marketing and Sales Enablement. We start each engagement off with a 1 hour free consultation to quickly see if they are a good fit for Inbound Marketing and Hubspot. We have found that this is the quickest and most effective way to help our clients succeed. That's why you should book your <u>1 hour free consultation</u> now. The time slots are filling up (which is by design).

---

63. This was around 2007, and Hubspot's founders, Brian Halligan and Dharmesh Shah had only just invented the phrase, so it is normal for such a new and novel concept to be largely unknown to a corporate behemoth like SAP.

Content is The Rocket Fuel

Of all the challenges you're likely to face when doing Inbound Marketing, developing high converting profitable content will be the number one challenge. You've either got to be both a Subject Matter Expert (SME) and able to develop it yourself, or you have to have the budget to have it developed for you. When we started our own Inbound Journey, Hubspot had not formally launched the Hubspot Partner program. This meant we were on own. Because we actually are SMEs within the world of SAP and now, Inbound Marketing, we were able to develop over 400 pieces of 'content'. Conservatively speaking, that's around one million dollars in content, should we have had someone develop it for us. We know that now because there are a number of websites where you can contract a writer to do it for you. Authoritative content, which is what we specialize in, is very expensive. We've also developed a number of online calculators that would start at around $35,000 and up to have developed. In addition, we've stretched the Hubspot tool set to develop advanced product selector and scoping tools, all of which are expensive, but high-performance tools.

Content Plan

There was one major issue with our approach – we didn't have a content plan. Nor did Hubspot have a content planning template. Today, as full fledged Hubspot partners, with many customer engagements under our belts, we've found that the critical success factor to customer success is having a published content plan.

There are two steps to developing a content plan:

- Performing a content audit
- Content Ideation

Given the extreme expense of creating new SEO Optimized, lead generation type content, the first step to getting your content in place is to take a look at what you already have. This includes doing a hard disk dump, (in an organized fashion), and looking at what you have out there on the internet already, i.e., YouTube. You may or may not be able to use this content as is, but it is a good starting place.

Step two to developing a content plan is to map your existing content to the Inbound Marketing Methodology Phases, using the content planning template. Assuming you already have your Buyer Persona identified, you now need to map the content to both Buyer Persona, Problems and Funnel Phase. Those phases are typically known as TOFU, MOFU, BOFU, or Top-of-the-Funnel, Middle-of-the-Funnel and Bottom-of-the-Funnel.

This is why we start with the Sales Funnel first, then work backwards, up the funnel. This content mapping process can take quite a while, and is never really done.

We always recommend to our clients that we build a complete top-to-bottom conversion funnel with at least one piece of content to start with. Build this content to the plan, create the related landing pages, thank you pages, blogs, social media posts, Smart Lists and Workflows, and you will have your first conversion funnel up and running. You will also have templates for each of these elements that you can easily clone[64] and reuse – a huge time saver down the line.

Some quick data points about content. Please keep in mind that there are literally millions of new blogs being published daily. That means it's highly competitive to rank. However, it is possible to rank organically, it just takes really high-quality content, in sufficient quantity, to get you there. Though there are no laws that say what those numbers have to be, it does appear that you need to have about 60 blogs published to get traction, and about 200 to be considered an authoritative website. Keep in mind, the core Inbound Marketing model offer is:

1. High-Quality Piece of downloadable or interactive content
2. Blog
3. Landing Page and Thank You page.

Some people write more than one blog to drive traffic to a single piece of content; and if the content deserves this level of blogging, by all means, do it. That downloadable piece of content, let's say it is a high quality 20 page whitepaper, will probably cost from $3,500 to $5,000 to have produced, though it can cost much more than that if it needs to be crafted by a deep industry expert. Why would that be? Because the deep industry expert is not usually also a skilled marketing content creation expert. Thus, you will find it takes a team effort to create high impact, high quality content. This is true whether you are producing a written piece of content or an online calculator or other tool.

---

[64]. Wordpress requires the addition of a plug-in to perform this task, and the actual 'cloned' result is never production ready.

In this author's experience, it typically takes me about 16 hours to draft a significant ebook, and another 6 hours to write a deep enough blog, and perhaps 2 hours to create the forms, landing pages, and copywriting of the landing page and thank you page. Pick whatever bill rate you like to work with, but 250 an hour is in the ballpark. However, I've worked with Sales Trainers who get 350 an hour, while copywriters like Ray Edwards may charge a quarter million dollars to do one Sales Page.

This excludes all the time to come up with the idea, which may require many hours of research using a variety of tools, like Google Trends, SEMRush, and other professional research. Many of these tools also have substantial associated subscription costs.

We're not saying you will need to produce 400 pieces of content, but we are saying you will need a lot, at least 60 pieces, but more likely 200. For those doing the math, you're looking at $1,200,000 over some period of time, but not a long period of time.

SEO and Paid For Content Distribution Amplification

If you produce high-quality level content, you'll want to do all you can to ensure it gets found by your potential customers. High quality SEO is, of course, a major part of making that happen. Google has other ideas. They want to make money, ostensibly because they want their users to find what they are looking for and to accomplish what they set out to do.

Paid Content Distribution

Google has many methods for you to advertise, collectively known as PPC advertising. There's a lot to know about doing it right, and we have managed millions in Google PPC advertising, so we've seen a thing or two.

You Pay More If You're Low Quality

You should know that besides all the setup you need to do to run Google ads successfully, Google will also be grading you, specifically, they will be assigning a grade to every page you send traffic to. The better your grade, the lower your advertising cost. What this actually translates to is that you need to make sure your website is a high converting website. The best converting web site page we've ever seen was based on a calculator. It was generating one new contact, every minute of every day, 1,440 a day, on a normal day. On peak days, when we also ran TV ads against it, it would generate up to 27,000 new contacts a day.

Normal Conversion Rates

This is not a normal conversion rate. You're going to be lucky to get from 5% to 20% as a conversion rate, possibly much less.

That's why you will need to find and fix absolutely every technical SEO element of your site and page, and you will never want to miss a lead, no matter how 'qualified' it may or may not be. You should know that Google's AI (Artificial Intelligence) system is way better than it was 5 years ago, or even a year ago. Of course, you need to understand how to create audiences, write ads, and do deep dive analytics. But as they advance their AI, they are getting much better at helping to optimize your ad spend.

Caveat: We've still not seen any machine learning system match what highly qualified, (read expensive) humans can achieve with Google PPC. The challenge was and is to create an offer that converts well, using content, whether it is something a user downloads, something a user does online, like a calculator, or some other clever offering. But if you get an offer that converts well and gets enough conversions on it to train the AI, then you can probably let it run, just keep an eye on the numbers. In one of our recent campaigns, where we scaled to about $135,000 a day ad-spend, we had a very aggressive target cost of acquisition target. The AI not only helped us meet our target, we actually came in well ahead of our target, adding more than spent to the bottom line. It had quite a ramp up time, but once it hit cruising altitude, we could safely pump money into it, being assured it was highly profitable.

Google isn't the only platform, but it does have the majority of the search market, when you count all their properties. Facebook, which owns Instagram and Whatsapp, among many systems, is the number two platform for paid content promotion. We've seen it work better than Google, but it depends on the offer and having the right Facebook Strategy. LinkedIn[65] is the major platform for B2B advertising, but it is vastly more expensive due to the extreme value of the targeting you do on LinkedIn.

Your content's ability to generate leads from organic traffic depends upon having your SEO elements, of which there are hundreds on every page, optimized. Each page, each offer, and your platform, all influence

---

[65]   Expensive is always relative to value. If you spend 1,000 dollars on a lead and make 1,000,000, it was not expensive. However, if you spend 100 dollars on a lead and it only generates 101 dollars in revenue, you probably lost money, but just can't track your cost close enough to realize it. Know your numbers.

your organic results, as well as all other traffic channels. SEO consulting is a skill that takes far more time and effort to develop than you may realize. It is also not something that is 'one and done'. It changes constantly, though Google officially will tell you, just produce high quality content and you will win. This may be true, but there are both technical, creative and functional aspects that have to be addressed to get SEO right so you show up on the first page of SERP (Search Engine Results Page) results.

Facebook

With two billion+ users on Facebook, it is impossible to ignore this social media channel. Perceived as a B2C or business-to-consumer platform, we have found that it works for just about every type of market. For instance, many of the largest SAP consultancies have a million or more followers on Facebook.

Hubspot offers integration into Facebook, specifically to the lead generation ad-type. This type of ad allows you to generate leads right within Facebook. However, to make Facebook work as a lead generation platform, you have to think social. That means you have to design a sales funnel that is driven within Facebook from top-to-bottom.

Facebook E-Commerce

For those in the e-commerce space, you can connect the Facebook platform to your store platform and have Facebook create audiences from the contacts visiting your store, and combine those audiences with content from your Inbound Marketing system to drive even greater results.

Facebook's Artificial Intelligence engine allows you to create look-alike audiences from these website audiences. That means it can find just the right user within its' user database and help you drive conversions.

Facebook also allows you to do e-commerce right within Facebook. This is a little used capability of the system, but we have had great success helping our clients sell via this channel. However, you don't have as much control over the 'look and feel' of the product pages a user sees within Facebook. This presents a challenge as far getting your 'brand' right within the Facebook platform.

Critical Success Factors

At the top of the list to getting Facebook to work for you profitably is to have a proven sales funnel within the right product or service niche. Cost of Customer Acquisition (CAC) is also critical here, as very low-priced products without a lot of up-sell or long-term customer value don't typically work well. On the other hand, many product categories work very well, think make-up, meal replacements, diet plans.

Having a properly installed and constantly monitored Facebook Pixel[66] installation with specific conversion events defined is another critical success factor. Though it is relatively easy to create your Facebook pixel and install it on a platform like Shopify, you're going to find that the pixel actually requires maintenance periodically, primarily when platform owners mess with their theme. Nothing will alert you to the fact that the pixel isn't firing or that what you had it set up to measure has been touched. For most 'code changes', you'll need a developer, but that is vaguely defined.

---

[66]. In order to obtain your Facebook Pixel, you will first need to set up your Facebook Business Manager, which is the tool you primarily use for Facebook advertising.

Designing and measuring your sales funnel[67] so that you can leverage Facebook Analytics is also a critical success factor. At the time of publication of this book, the Facebook Analytics system is still undergoing rapid changes, and sometimes displays erratic behavior, for instance, we've seen meticulously designed sales funnels just disappear from the Analytics Tool.

Researching your audiences and identifying interest so you can precisely target the right audience is one of the critical tasks of using Facebook Ads successfully. Although the Facebook AI has plenty of data to eventually get you to the exact target you're looking for, it can get expensive while it learns who to target. Take my word for it and help it along. I've yet to see any automated platform's AI outperform a human on this platform. But what it can do is get to 'good enough' so you can just let it run.

Success on Facebook goes way beyond just getting the technical side set up properly and running ads. It requires you to know and engage with your audience and be social. This means it takes real people expending real time[68] on the platform. You'll need to expend real dollars to make this happen. For large brands, who may have a lot of internal barriers to communication[69] with their true public, this can be a challenge.

---

67. Facebook Analytics allows you to design and monitor your sales funnel.
68. It is shocking how many entrepreneurs think this should be a free activity. It is not, and will only get more expensive.
69. Until the advent of systems like Hubspot, most large brands neither had customer contact information nor wanted it. That has dramatically changed with the success of e-commerce platforms like Amazon.

YouTube

The video platform watched by the entire planet, is also an amazing lead generation machine, but you have to know how to use it. Owned by Google, you can run e-commerce ads below your videos[70] or those of your competitors. You can also create your own tribe on YouTube. Driven by comments and other social proof signals, many channels accumulate thousands or even millions of subscribers and millions or even billions[71] of views, all of which provide a place to advertise.

Many, if not most YouTube viewers, at least the ones of most value to the typical business, are of the "How To" type[72]. But many other viewers watch many other types of videos. The only way to find out what will work for you is to test it.

You can, of course, also earn revenue from your own YouTube videos, but we have not seen this be a major revenue source for most of our clients. But we have seen a lot of leads and sales generated from this channel.

One thing most business owners' may not realize is that though YouTube videos may generate a lot of views, for the most part, they drive views away from your site and onto YouTube. To verify this yourself, go to www. google.com/videos then type in a video of yours that is hosted on YouTube but embedded on your site. Take a look at the link. It most probably links to YouTube. My recommendation is to exploit both video channels (actually, all video channels, which can include Facebook, Instagram, Vimeo, and even Hubspot).

[70.] Currently known as Tru-View ads
[71.] For example, Despacito, has 6.5 billion views and counting as of the writing of this book.
[72.] For beginning advertising, we usually recommend going with How To, but there are exceptions to the rule.

YouTube Use Cases

We've seen some traction with YouTube live events and TruView Advertising. In the first instance, we've helped clients do everything from simple product unboxings to studio setup's and doing 2 hours of live broadcasting with guest, scripts and skits. YouTube videos are different from TV broadcast in that people can view them long after the broadcast. In fact, the older the video is, the more views it has likely accumulated. Of course, if you have a massively viral video, and it is monetized, you could make a good return just from the video. For many YouTube stars, this is their primary revenue model. For e-commerce based product sellers, it is really more about the messaging than anything.

TruView, a relatively new Google offering, gives you the possibility of having your shoppable product appear in ads below your video. This used to be limited to a very short list of retailers but Google opened it up recently and it seems to represent a major new sales channel.

Wistia

This is one of 2 video platforms that have deep integration with Hubspot[73]. They are not the same as YouTube or Vimeo in the sense they aren't really a platform with a large viewership. But they are ideal in two particular use cases:

By hosting your video on Wistia and embedding your video on your website, you will get Google SEO credit, whereas if you embed a YouTube hosted video on your site, you are sending your Google SEO juice

---

[73.] Integration is a driving theme for much of what we recommend. It often is the key differentiator among the different systems

to YouTube, another Google property. If you want to verify this, embed a YouTube video on your site and search for it using Google.com/video. Notice where the link is?

Wistia itself is simple to use. However, it isn't quite as simple as just upload a video, grab the embed code and insert. It uses the 'Project' concept, and in addition to providing a place for you to create video meta data, it also allows for collaboration among team members when setting it up.

The real value it provides, aside from Video SEO juice, is the ability to capture leads. You've probably seen these forms that appear on a video a few minutes into it asking you to submit your email to continue viewing. Those emails can be directly fed into your email service provider, like MailChimp or most importantly, into Hubspot.

This is where the real magic happens. You can create branching logic with Hubspot's workflow tool to send people down different routes to different videos, depending on where they watched to in your video. I've seen some major results with clients of mine using Wistia. In one instance, the client had 250 gigabytes of videos, including countless recorded customer sessions, which they had permission to use, but had not.

By simply turning on the lead capture form capability, updating the Video SEO and actually having someone follow-up on these leads, he captured an additional $500,000 in revenue – in about 2 months.

You don't have to be a Hollywood film producer to make videos that work. You do have to tell a story. You probably do that all day long. Whip out your iPhone and record some of those conversations. They are gold.

Vidyard

This is a video hosting platform that allows you to record and embed videos right from within Hubspot using a Chrome add-on. This is especially powerful when you are sending sales-oriented emails. People want to see who you are and how you're saying whatever it is you're saying.

Keep your email videos to under 3 minutes, as most people will not watch them all the way through. The only exception is if you're an exceptionally accomplished public speaker. Just make sure your story is worth the listen.

I also recommend you stand up when you record a video, whether on Vidyard or any other platform. If you have the choice, get a lavalier microphone and deliver your spiel with your hands in full motion. It changes the message content and tone your receiver perceives, even if you don't think so.

If you're an accomplished public speaker, by all means, put that skill to use here and other places or any stage you can get on. If you're not, practice makes perfect. There are also some great courses available on LinkedIN Learning[74]. Or you might consider joining Toastmasters[75] or even a theater. If you want to double your revenue, become a master communicator, in all channels.

---

[74]. You usually must have a LinkedIN Premium Account to take these courses. I find they are excellent courses.

[75]. Toastmasters is an organization that promotes the development of public speaking skills. They have chapters all over the world.

Amazon

Just about all of our e-commerce clients either sell or want to sell on Amazon or should sell on Amazon. Makes sense, since they are the 800 pound Gorilla in the e-commerce space. It's fairly straight forward to get up and running on Amazon. At least it is for us now. It definitely wasn't easy when we started. Fortunately, they provide training[76] for everything you need to know in their seller university, which is really a series of instructional videos that are arranged in the order you should be following as you set up your store.

Critical Success Factors

Have Products That People Want to Buy

Probably above everything else you have to get right in order to successfully sell on Amazon, you have to select your product carefully. If it sells well on your own store, then it probably will sell well on Amazon.

Use Fulfillment by Amazon (FBA).

Known by consumers as Amazon prime, we've seen conversion rates as high as 60%, but we typically see it hover between 20 and 30 percent. This is drastically higher than the typical 1 or 2 percent average conversion rate you get on an e-commerce store. You should know you first have to be invited by Amazon to participate in FBA, which usually comes after a few months of successfully selling products using Merchant Fulfillment,

---

[76.]   All of Amazon's training is available via their online Sellers University.

which means sold on Amazon, but shipped by you from your own warehouse, which might be a garage or a 3rd party logistics provider or 3PL.

Seller Fulfilled Prime

Once you're able to meet strict performance standards, you may be invited to participate in what is currently called, on the backend of Amazon, Seller Fulfilled Prime. Users will see this as Merchant Fulfilled Prime. What it means in practice is that Amazon wants merchants to provide free shipping and meet very tight delivery deadlines. This means you have to have shipped a lot of product all over the United States so you have some data about each carrier's ability. You then will have to update (or really, you copy and update an existing shipping template) your existing shipping template to reflect SFP delivery zones. This is not an easy process and requires careful consideration of whether it makes sense financially from the seller's perspective.

Meeting FBA Performance Demands.

The part you have to keep in mind with FBA is that you have to keep inventory in Amazon's warehouse, and when they make a sale on your behalf, they will ship directly from their warehouse. There are a number of financial issues you have to contend with here. One is the cost of inventory you're going to have to keep on-hand in Amazon's warehouse. But in order for Amazon to meet their shipping and delivery commitments to their Amazon prime members, they will need to keep your inventory in multiple locations, which means you will need more inventory. The faster they sell, the more often you will need to resupply Amazon.

Keep in mind, you will be paying a fee to Amazon to store your inventory as well as fulfill your orders. That's the key reason you have to know every single penny of this set up. Amazon wants you to be successful, but not too successful. What this means is, especially for new, unproven suppliers, they have to be convinced you can meet their sales volumes. If you have a product you've launched and it is getting, say, 50 sales a month, they aren't going to give you orders for 100,000 sales a month, even if they have the traffic to do it (they do and I will tell you how you can figure that out a little later on). If you let your FBA items go zero balance, you will notice that your sales do not automatically recover immediately when you resupply. That's because they have a massive demand generation machine that keeps generating product searches no matter whether you have fulfillable stock on-hand or not. They pay a tremendous amount of money to create this demand and won't waste clicks on a product that isn't in stock. It just that smart of a system.

Scouting Out Sales Figures

When you're evaluating Amazon as a potential sales channel, you'll need a tool to help you find what particular items are both selling for as well as the estimated monthly sales volume. There are several available, but a good one is called Amazon Scout, which is available as an extension on Google Chrome (in both a free and paid version). Like all things free, it has limited but useful functionality. If you have the cash, not a bad investment.

Subscribe and Save

If your product is one that people can subscribe to, and if it can be, you should definitely sign-up for the program, then you will have a whole new set of performance metrics to track. For some items, like coffee, consumers will happily sign up for monthly deliveries, especially Amazon Prime members. For the vendor, it means they have to have enough inventory on hand to meet these automatic renewals. Sadly, the reporting isn't great as far as telling vendors which products, in which quantity, on which dates, will be demanded from Subscribe and Save customers. But it is buried in the reports.

Major Challenges

Listing Creation

Creating a listing on Amazon using one of their product upload templates is a near constant challenge. For products that have parent child relationships, size selections to be made or color selections (there are many other examples of variants), getting all the data formatted correctly so it works can be frustrating. The good news is, once you get one to work, each time you do it after that, with a new product, it generally works, unless they've updated the template, which they do, frequently.

GTIN Numbers

Like all retailers, Amazon uses GTIN (Global Trade Item Numbers) numbers, which are fairly expensive to buy. If you're just starting out, you probably won't have one for each product. This is a major issue for which you will need to seek a waiver from Amazon in order to use the upload template approach. You will, however, need UPC codes if you are going to utilize FBA. You can buy your own through any number of providers or you can buy them from Amazon. This second option is fairly expensive, while the first option means you have to know how to incorporate the UPC image into your labels. That usually means you're going to need a label printer, of which only a few work really well.

Creating Quality Listings

For each product type, Amazon provides a Style Guide which you must follow, especially with regards to product photos. Of course, you must get all elements of your product description just right to make them sell. Aside from the customer facing part of quality listings, there is a whole world of behind-the-scenes elements you need to get right for Amazon to find your product. Here's where you need to make sure you get your product titles exactly right, your 'About this Product' exactly right, and your search terms.

Depending on your product, there are a whole host of other data elements you'll need to get right, all of which Amazon's algorithm uses in returning the right product to the right customer at the right time. In short, this isn't an area where you get to take a short cut. Don't expect too much help from Amazon personnel here, either, unless you're a major seller. For the small guy, expect only perfunctory email based FAQs. The answer may or may not be there, but you will burn a lot of your time working your way through this process, until you get it right. This is one of the areas where experience is worth paying for, which doesn't come cheap and is limited in availability.

A quality listing also means having all the fields in the product backend completed. Particularly the size and weight information. This is what Amazon bases their storage fees on and thus, for tight margin, slow moving products, this can wipe out your profit margin.

Catalog Data Feeds.

If you have a large number of products, you may find yourself using a data feed[77]. There are third-party systems, such as Shoppingfeeder that provide these. You can also do it manually using carefully formatted CSV files. What you should be aware of is that these data feeds actually form a critical information juncture between your online store and other marketplaces, like Amazon or Google Merchant Center. In order to run sales, and what store doesn't run a constantly changing mixture of sales, the datafeed has to be set up to support these sales or your customers won't be aware of the sales. Practically speaking, it means you'll have to monitor this on a regular basis to ensure it is up-to-date with sales, seasonality and events, among many things.

For very large retailers, the Open Catalog Interface or OCI, which is supported by major ERP vendors, such as SAP, can be used to feed their product information to Amazon. The challenge here is the same for a large vendor as it is for a small vendor – accuracy of information. Amazon relies on accurate inventory information to make delivery calculations, and suppliers who run afoul of their rules can and have been summarily dropped from the platform.

Business-to-Business or B2B

If at all possible, and if your product fits in the B2B space, then you should also be selling on the B2B side of Amazon. Within the Amazon backend, you will see it in your menu, and underneath that menu, a whole new world will open up for you to work through. It's fairly straight forward to use. The important thing to

---

[77.] There are a number of Data Feed providers, each with differing capabilities as well as cost. You can also use a CSV file for small, slowly changing items, but you will waste an enormous amount of time going this route.

keep in mind here is that it is a channel directly into the purchasing departments of many businesses. How is that so? Because many businesses have corporate accounts with Amazon, which is in turn, integrated with the business' procurement department. This means that instead of you, a tiny business, trying to become a certified vendor to each and every corporation you want to sell to, you are, instead, piggybacking off of Amazon's existing approved vendor status with a huge number of businesses.

For instance, say your office consumes coffee, as many do. They can either send someone down to the grocery store to buy more, which isn't really a great solution, or go online and order from Amazon. They'll most likely get volume discounts and you, the vendor, will move more product. So don't let this channel lay idle.

You can also run B2B specific promotions using this channel. You use the same tools to set these up as you would to run a promotion on the B2C side of Amazon.

Shopify

You may be wondering how a group of SAP consultants who specialize in Hubspot came to know about Shopify. The backstory: The author had been hired by television personality, Alejandro Chaban, to run his Hubspot system. What does an SAP Consultant know about television personalities? Nothing. At least not when I got hired for that project. Alejandro Chaban, founder of the Yes You Can! Diet Plan, had built a wildly successful e-commerce operation using Hubspot, Salesforce and Zuora, with a lot of other systems as well, including a custom-built shopping cart, in about 3 years. The problem was, the marketing consultants who had helped in the past, didn't really know Hubspot and had broken it. When I came onboard, the system was barely functioning and the client was unaware that the Hubspot to Salesforce integration was not working, nor that tens of thousands of contacts were not being passed to the call center to be worked.

Among many tasks undertaken by this author on this project, was to evaluate possible replacement solutions for the existing e-commerce platform, which required outside programmers on a constant basis to maintain and make the constant changes testing was telling us to make. My team and I evaluated all the major e-commerce platforms, concluding ultimately that Shopify with a subscription application would more than serve their needs. We were asked to do a proof-of-concept or POC with our target architecture, so I had to learn all of these platforms, set them up in a sandbox[78], and deliver the POC. Thus we learned way more about Shopify than we set out to do. We're glad we got this experience.

Shopify is a leading e-commerce platform with over 1 million subscribers and more than 1,000 applications available within the Shopify eco-system. There are 4 different Shopify Platform subscription levels[79], starting as low as 9 dollars a month all the way up to the enterprise version that runs $2,000 a month. (All pricing is, as of the publication of this book, subject to change at any time by Shopify).

We've now done enough Shopify e-commerce projects that involved both Hubspot and Shopify that we have a highly refined on-boarding process. We have taken a number of companies from no online e-commerce presence up to steady-state run rates with a complex set of applications installed and working together.

---

78. A sandbox is the same thing as a test environment.
79. Subscription level means how much you pay per month to use their system. These prices do not include transaction fees.

Critical Success Factors

SEO or Search Engine Optimization

If you're starting from zero sales and zero traffic, the challenge will be to get to the first sale. Getting your SEO right is, of course, a requirement. There's a lot to know and get right. At a high-level, you'll need to get your Page Name, URL, Meta Descriptions, Product Descriptions, Product Images and Alt Tags, Videos, Social Media, Ratings, Content Offerings, and technical issues, such as site speed, schema.org tags and ALL tracking codes, set up correctly. There is the initial pass at this and then the on-going SEO efforts, which are driven by Google changes as well as changing consumer behavior. In short, this may be the easiest money you'll make, but it is also one of the ones where you'll likely have to spend a lot of time getting it right. Top end SEO consultants[80] can and do charge top rates. We've never found this to be something that can be successfully off-shored. It simply requires too much knowledge of your customer's culture and product to really get it right. We don't expect this aspect to change anytime soon.

Product Descriptions

Writing product descriptions that sell is as much about proper structure as it is about finding the emotional triggers a product should hit. Technically, product descriptions, like all other parts of the system, are part of the SEO. They are also what Google will use when you run Product Listing Ads (PLA). Of course, they are

---

[80.] At this point in my career, I am considered a top end SEO consultant. But it took almost 10 years of training and experience to get to this level.

what customers are going to read and evaluate your product with. There are three golden rules I follow when writing a product description:

- Clarity and Conciseness
- Benefits due to Features
- Storytelling

This means being very clear about what is being offered, explaining the benefits and the features that the product has that yields those benefits, and wrapping it up with a story.

Beyond the basic product description, you should also be blogging. For instance, if you sell shoes, you probably aren't going to be able to write a lot of blogs about shoes. But you can write a lot of blogs about a subject that surrounds the product or for which the product is a part of. For instance, if you sell weight lifting shoes, you can write on all the different aspect of weightlifting, bodybuilding, nutrition, and training. To get consistent results, you need a lot of blogs, specifically, it seems to take about 60 blogs to start seeing results, while at around 200, you become a trusted source.

At one of my clients, we had over 1000 blogs, which were generating over 1,000,000 pages views[81] a month! In fact, we published 2 blogs a day, in English and Spanish, 7 days a week. Many of those blogs were subsequently repurposed by converting them into downloadable ebooks, which generated many thousands of additional customers.

[81.] Page Views are often called vanity metrics, but we had a clear conversion rate from page views to customer. For us, more page views meant more customers, at a predictable rate.

Nailing the 4 P's

Shopify isn't magic. For it to truly deliver the goods, you will need to nail the classic 4 P's of marketing, Product, Price, Place, Promotion, much like you would with any other approach to marketing and sales. We've had to deliver the 'tough love' to more than a few clients that their price is too high, even though they believe they're unique and special. It's not a challenge to research 30 to 60 similar products on Amazon and see what the real selling price should be. What's more, there are tools you can use to get sales figures from Amazon for just about every product they sell. They are useful to help formulate your pricing strategy.

Because you'll most likely be using Shopify as your central e-commerce platform, connect to a wide array of sales channels, such as Amazon, Facebook, Instagram, E-Bay, Etsy, Pinterest, POS, Messenger and many others, you'll be in a lot of 'Places', but not all will work for your product. You will need to try them out, but sooner rather than later, cull the dogs.

Promotion will be where your real challenge comes from. Your pricing cannot and will not be static. You'll need to develop a discount strategy, an email promotional strategy (this is a key channel) and a discount strategy for each channel. It will be a never ending challenge to truly have a 360 degree view of each customer, though with the vigilant use of Google UTM codes, you will have very good data within Google Analytics. The Shopify store comes with good but limited analytics. There are reporting packages[82] available too greatly enhance your analytics and if the numbers work, you should install it. They are not inexpensive.

[82.] As a general rule of thumb, we find most Shopify stores end up with from 15 to 25 add-on software packages when their store is fully optimized.

Inventory Management

For most of our smaller clients, this is a major weak spot. They want to design and sell their product. If you're strictly a drop-shipper, this mostly isn't a big issue. We mostly deal with stores that design, manufacture and sell their own brands of products. Sometimes, they design and produce 'white label' for others. Typically, the product is designed in the U.S. and produced in China. That means you have a supply chain to manage and most critically, dollars are going to be tied up in inventory. Let's say you've been in business for a while and have determined that it takes 80 days from the time you issue a purchase order until the product hits your shelf and is ready for sale. If you sell, say 250 units a month, and your inventory resupply is for 500 units, it means every 2 months you will need to resupply, which is 6 times a year you're going to need a bucket of cash. If sales increase, you may run out of inventory before you receive new inventory. If sales don't quite meet expectations, you may find you have more inventory on hand than desired (and cash tied up in that inventory).

On the other hand, if you run out of inventory, every visit you generate to your website will convert at ever lower rates, if at all. Google knows how you're doing. If their users aren't buying on your site, because you're out of stock, your traffic will magically disappear, while your cost of paid advertising will go up as punishment for disappointing a user.

Getting inventory levels right is no mean feat. That's why Supply Chain Management was and is a well-paid field which involves some complex IT systems and sometimes, even more complex math. We all want to operate on a Just-In-Time or JIT inventory level, but as has been noted, when you lower inventory levels, much like when you lower water levels in a lake, rocks begin to show. When you increase inventory velocity, you get the same effect, rocks just below the surface cause ripples in your flow.

Inventory management is not and will never be a one and done affair. For the one man army, or a vast, complex enterprise, this is an area of critical importance which must be managed constantly.

Product Pictures

Having high quality product pictures, including videos and gifs, is a 'must have' for success on not just Shopify but any e-commerce platform. Your customers cannot touch the product, so images must serve as the stand in for touching it. Want to know a secret. For virtually every product category, Amazon provides a Style Guideline that usually includes sample pictures. They aren't in there in just any random order. They are in the order they are in, presented the way they are, because Amazon has tested them. You should probably use their guidelines for your Shopify images, and add lifestyle shots sparingly. It's ok and recommended to use the lifestyle images to provide your store with some unique personality. But our experience indicates, use the proven Amazon style guides.

You should plan on investing in what is called a light box if you are going to produce product images yourself, ideally with a product turntable built in. These are basically white boxes with lighting that allows you to create the Apple style infinite image with no shadows. The turnstile allows you to create rotating images. These can be very visually appealing if professionally rendered.

There are, of course, service bureaus who do this work. Just make sure they have the proper capability and can follow explicit instructions. Otherwise, you're in for some long, disappointing engagements.

Break-Even Analysis

One of the most important metrics a store owner needs to know is his Breakeven 'unit' and 'sales' number. Now you might be asking yourself whether a marketing and sales expert should be concerned with something so clearly within the financial management domain. The answer is, in our experience, that unless you know the financials, the store will constantly want to change the marketing mix, when, in fact, it's doing fine and the problems lie elsewhere in the business, probably within the supply chain.

Be forewarned, though this calculation is very simple to do, it can be a challenge to collect the data. When you're first starting out, you won't have much data about fixed cost. That's why you will need to estimate your fixed costs and then as you get additional real data, update your assumptions. It's also why you need to connect Shopify to your accounting package, typically Quickbooks. But Quickbooks, though it can explain how you compute this number in a blog, it won't actually provide it to you. So, excel will be involved somewhere along the line. That's all right, as it provides a robust 'what if' capability that is easy to use and many people know how to use excel. We provide a free download of a Break-Even analysis spreadsheet[83] that we developed for own in-house use.

Contribution Margin

Defined as how much each unit of sales is available to cover fixed cost, the formula for Contribution Margin is simply Sales Revenue – Variable Cost. Normally, when conducting a break-even analysis, you go ahead and determine your contribution margin. When you have multiple SKUs, you have to perform a slightly more

---

[83].   We have recently converted this to an online calculator at the request of several users.

complicated version of multi-unit break even analysis that involves using weighted average sales of each item. Sounds complicated but with a spreadsheet, you can easily do it. If you have a years' worth a data, it may be sufficient to just stick with a simple Contribution Margin. Knowing and using these two KPIs will allow you to know just how much you can and should be spending on marketing and advertising. In essence, this tells you how close to the Sun you can fly as far spending on marketing and promotion goes.

Major Challenges

Though Shopify is a robust, simple to use system, there is no guarantee you will make any sales. The competition, after all, is fierce. That said, getting traffic to your store will be one of if not the, major challenges you will face. We've already covered the necessity of getting your SEO right. But in order for you to make sales, you're going to need content. Lots of it. The primary way to do that is to write blogs. There are other ways, such as developing online calculators and other web based tools. But the proven way is to write blogs.

Most business owners don't have the time or writing chops to churn out high quality blogs in sufficient numbers to move the needle on traffic. Like a normal Inbound Marketing focused website, you will need to have anywhere from 60 blogs (on the extreme low-end) to 200 (we've seen 400 to 1000 be the magic number for certain product categories) to really generate a steady increase in organic traffic.

Synchronizing your inventory with Amazon can also prove to be a major challenge. This is done via an electronic connection available from Shopify and in theory, should work fine. It rarely does. Expect to spend some of your time on this subject on an on-going basis especially if you run frequent sales and or deal with highly configurable products and services.

Interactive Online Content Creation

Given the extreme saturation[84] of the digital marketing space with content, consumers now demand an ever-higher level of engagement from the content they do decide to consume. Interactive content is the new Gold Standard. It includes things such as calculators, quizzes, assessment tools, interactive video, sizing tools, and any number of other tools that allow consumers to generate their own answers, which becomes UGC or User Generated Content.

For many businesses, with just a little imagination, you can come up with an idea for a calculator. For example, we wanted to know how do you decide on your call center staffing levels[85]. We had the opportunity of working with a Call Center that ran on Salesforce+Hubspot and had about 160 call center agents in 2 different geographic locations. We were able to develop an online calculator that tells you exactly how many call center employees you will need.

Other interesting interactive tools we've developed are product selection tools using just Hubspot and Smart List. For example, we built a tool to help our clients select the right Hubspot subscription. This tool was developed due to the complexity we encountered with each new client when it came time to select the appropriate tools

There are also several applications out there (whose number is growing) to help you develop interactive tools. These include SnapApp, Ceros, RSM Video, and Tumult Hype, among our favorites. Of course, a developer

---

[84] Millions of blogs are published everyday, as an example of saturation.

[85] This calculation is typically done by the Call Center Manager using largely unwritten rules of thumb, until we wrote them down, turned it into a calculation using queue theory, and created the online calculator.

can build a calculator from scratch, but that can get very expensive, and takes some time. With a tool like SnapApp, it is possible to generate a calculator in a few minutes that offers very sophisticated functionality. Like all tools, you need to do the training on it before diving in, but you can quickly build more calculators once you get the hang of it.

Before you go building a calculator, you should first see if it is going to answer a question that customers actually want to know the answer too. We've built 17 different interactive tools for our own use on SAPBWConsulting. com and not all have been resounding successes. Others have performed beyond expectations. With each iteration, we have slowly uncovered the 'rules of the road' when it comes to developing these tools successfully:

- Does the tool allow you to answer a question uniquely – in other words, has it already been done by another website.
- Is the information encapsulated within the tool unique IP (Intellectual Property) to your business?
- Can you build it in excel to start with?

Anytime we have had a prospect ignore these rules, their calculator has not performed well. We have also seen calculators that were directly responsible for generating $4,000,000 a month in revenue by answering a question that was already answered elsewhere by at least 100 other websites.

Gamifying your interactive tool, as is widely done by video game designers, is also a powerful technique for building successful online tools. People love to win, so build a system where they can and you will make more money.

Sales

We've already mentioned the importance of knowing what you sell. Most businesses are either in the process of developing a sales process or updating a sales process. Let's take SAP, which is over 40 years old. They have an army of sales people and spend massively on marketing, including Inbound Marketing. In 2001, they launched ValueSAP™, and introduced a concept called Customer Engagement Lifecycle or CEL for short. In 2008, it got a significant facelift with the introduction of Value Engineering[86] and the establishment of Business Transformation Services.

In 2012, deep into the financial crisis, they started focusing on selling their cloud-based HANA® (High Performance Analytic Application) solution. Each of these transition points required the provision of a repeatable sales process which could be followed by the sales team.

While they were and are constantly adjusting their approach, their competitors were also doing the same thing. That's why there is a such a huge market for Sales Trainers. Without taking an engineering approach to the sales process, hiring and training the right sales people and making sure the sales team is following the steps in your defined sales process, failure is the only possible outcome.

Their transition to focus on the cloud seems to be working, as evidenced by their annual report. But if you look at back issues of their annual report, say, starting with 1999 and then dipping your toes in about every 5 years, you come to realize they aren't selling ERP, their core system, all that much anymore. They are, instead, selling a variety of software solutions they have acquired, while extending the core out into 'white

---

86. Value Engineering is not a term unique to SAP. The term has long been used by many organizations, including the U.S. Government.

spaces[87]'. This is really due to a couple of major 'market' issues, one, they have already sold to most of the large companies, and a lot of the small and mid-size companies, and two, the wide spread adoption of high-speed internet connectivity globally has meant a lot of companies are focusing on other issues.

These business environment changes have driven changes not just to the solution SAP offers, but has meant they have had to continuously adjust their sales strategy, or what they refer to as Go-to-Market (GTM).

Not all businesses have the resources that an SAP class company has. For many smaller enterprises, right on down to the one-man army, they are on their own.

That's also an advantage, because they can move fast and are forced to figure out how to leverage digital marketing and sales to be successful.

Where Do We Recommend You Start?

Build from the sales transaction backwards. If you're in the service business world, which is about 80% of the businesses out there, you need to create your contracts up front. Though you will, of course, always be told to seek the advice of a lawyer when it comes to contracts, we will tell you, don't let a lawyer write your sales contracts. They should review what you write and understand. They shouldn't advise you on Sales Contract language strategy, but rather, just make sure you're not doing anything illegal and most importantly, not opening up you or your company to a liability that you could or should avoid.

[87.] The definition of 'white spaces' is fluid. In this context, it means where a solution exist within the SAP Solution Set, yet it is not being sold within client accounts to cover required functionality that it could cover. It is also used to identify spaces where SAP could develop a solution if the market was attractive to SAP commercially.

Within the Consulting space, there is, frankly speaking, a lot of bullying going on. The big guys will virtually always try to cram their contract down your throat when they are buying from you and tell you it is take or leave it. Don't be deceived. All contracts and all contract elements can and should be negotiated. We do it all the time. They no more want to spend money on lawyers than you do.

For those in the consulting space, there is, sadly, a lot of paperwork. But if you break it down, what you will find is really 2 documents: The Master Services Agreement (MSA) or as it is sometimes called the Professional Services Agreement (PSA) and the Statement of Work (SOW). For many scenarios, you will also be asked to sign an NDA or Non-Disclosure Agreement, which typically comes before either the MSA or PSA. It is also possible to incorporate the NDA into either of these documents.

The MSA is used to set the ground rules of the relationship while the SOW is used to actually define the 'who' and 'what' of the task at hand, along with pricing, payments, and anything else that needs to be detailed out, like who pays expenses.

You Need a CPQ System

Creating and sending Quoting and Closing documents for the deal is still mostly a manual process, even though most IT Companies, including SAP and Hubspot, are in the business of automating such things. Don't despair, we've coupled a CPQ (Configure, Price and Quote) system called Pandadoc with Hubspot which allows us to store these key documents for ready use. In short, we turned the Professional Services market into an e-commerce enabled market. We've been closing deals using this approach for quite a while now, and have learned a lot along the way.

There is no easy way to create these documents, it just takes clear headed thinking, well written (meaning easily understood) contracts and the use of digital technology to get it all online. However, there are templates available and, in our case, we had hundreds of previous engagements to develop our models from.

The reason I went into detail on this is that this approach is scalable. We are able to use our systems to deploy consultants anywhere in the world in any currency and handle all the sales transaction and execution paperwork electronically. This is a far cry from the days when it was excel and paper receipts taped to a white sheet of paper for review by the accounting department. This approach is both scalable and helps you win more deals, faster.

Taking this design approach one step further, we've been able to help SAP Partners move to a subscription based model for remote consulting support. To get to this sales model required an onsite workshop with the entire team to walk through their offering and 'uncover' the math behind their offering, something they had struggled with up to that point in time. Uncovering the true offering is a challenge most every business faces, but if you follow a logical process, you can get there.

What about other non-SAP type businesses? How should they approach their sales process? Work from the sales transaction backwards. For example, an e-commerce store needs to make sure people can actually checkout on their platform. We've run across a significant number of e-commerce stores where we've discovered people could not easily checkout, especially on mobile. You may have noticed that a lot of people use a mobile phone these days. If you know anything at all about e-commerce, you will have noticed that about 80% of your traffic is mobile while a lesser amount results in a conversion. That's why you have to get that part right.

For many companies, buying online from another company remains off-limits due to previous rules. But they are still shopping on your site. That's why you have to provide a way to facilitate a transaction over the phone, which is usually done within your e-commerce system, but paid via Invoice. For large dollar transactions, this makes sense. But for smaller size orders, you may want to just kill that approach altogether and work on making your sales transaction seamless. After all, the same companies that are throwing sand in your gears by trying to dictate their terms as buyers to you are often times trying to improve the process of their customers. Just takes designing your sales process to be an engineered step-by-step process.

Your Sales Funnel

In the process of designing your sales funnel, which is really just another way of saying, your sales process, you will see a need to provide defined actions for each stage of the funnel. There is an inherent conflict between Sales and Marketing when it comes to designing and using a sales funnel. Marketing is usually the only people concerned with the top of the funnel, unless sales is generating its own leads. But marketing actually has to work with Sales at every stage of the funnel to understand what is working. They need to produce content for customers to support each stage of the sales funnel as customers go on their journey through your sales funnel.

What works best here as far as designing your sales funnel? It helps a lot if you have some conversion rates to work with already. A full up sales and marketing funnel will typically have the following 'theoretical steps"

1. Website Visits
2. Contact
3. Leads

4. Marketing Qualified Lead

5. Sales Qualified Lead

6. Opportunity

7. Close

8. Delight

It all seems very complicated, doesn't it? There are only 2 'optional' steps in this funnel, steps 4 and 5, Marketing and Sales qualified leads. But we recommend you keep them in your funnel. They invariably lead to a little conflict when it comes to defining them and getting everybody to agree to the definition. Trust us on this, those are real steps, and you will need them. If you're just starting out, these steps can be difficult to identify.

It is with these Sales Funnel steps that you can really leverage the power of the Hubspot Inbound Marketing platform. It allows you to connect each stage of your funnel using email and social media. Steps 1 through 4 belong to marketing, while 5 through 7 belong to Sales. Step 8 belongs to the company, no matter what department they work in.

When using this approach, we find it best to define your steps on sticky notes, and then lay them out against the stages on a wall. After you're happy with the design of each step at each funnel stage, then you can set up your website with all the required pages, smart list[88], workflows and emails required to acquire, nurture and close leads all the way through to deal closure. As a side effect, you will also have the information you need

---

[88].   Smart Lists, at least within the world of Hubspot, are list created when someone converts on a website, and the list dynamically updates as more people convert. There are other types of list as well, such as Static List.

to measure not just discrete point-in-time funnel conversion rates, but as you make changes, you will gain an idea of how your improvement efforts are paying off for your entire process.

Marketing Process Design

If you start by designing your Sales Funnel, much of the work of designing your marketing process will have already been done, or at least you will have a framework you can follow as you build out your strategy.

This book is all about how to dominate any market using digital marketing and sales. Though there are a variety of marketing platforms out there, we believe Hubspot is currently the best choice and are writing this book based on you having all of the capabilities[89] of the system available to you.

Without the full suite of Hubspot capabilities, it is not going to be easy, effective or cheap to accomplish much with digital marketing. Sure, you can put up a Frankensite using Wordpress, sure you can put in Google Analytics. Trust us on this, when you get done knitting together all the systems you're going to need to do Inbound Marketing, you will have a Frankenstein on your hands and in all likelihood, won't see much of a payoff from your efforts. There are always exceptions to this rule, but the Hubspot system is a highly developed, super simple to use system designed by and for marketers. As jaded SAP consultants, we're impressed with it.

---

89.   It is possible to knit together kludged version of Hubspot using Wordpress and many, many plugins.

Your Process Is Never Done

Once you have fully defined each stage of your marketing funnel, you're going to need marketing content. There are a wide variety of content types, with an almost infinite number of 'guru's out there telling you what to do.

Here's what you need to keep in mind – marketing is never 'done'. Content you produced today, even if meant to be evergreen, will eventually stop working and need to be updated or replaced. One of the most helpful documents you can create as part of designing your marketing process is to define, using qualitative and quantitative methods, your customer journey. This can be quite involved, cost considerable money and take a while. It is one of the best investments you will make.

Your Customer Journey Will Change Over Time

You will make many assumptions about your customer's journey during the design process. As you ramp up your marketing efforts and gather more and more data, you should be revising your customer journey map. One great 'best practice' is to purchase something from your business, and record every step, including taking delivery of the product or service and actually using it or setting it up. Conversion Rate Optimization or CRO depends heavily upon this approach. It's how you become a data driven organization and can be done for any size organization and just about every type of service, including complex IT projects.

Call Center

For many businesses, they will have a call center[90], often times, many interconnected call centers. In most cases where the author has worked to optimize the Call Center setup, there is almost always a combination of overseas and US based call centers, linked by software, such as Salesforce.

A call center cost a lot of money to operate, but we find that humans have a higher close rate than automated sales processes – but only under certain conditions and only with the right training and mentorship.

An Inbound Approach Coupled With an Outbound Call Center is Powerful

For truly outstanding sales performance, we have found that when you have a high performance Inbound Lead generation platform, such as Hubspot, coupled with a High-Volume Call Center, typically ran on top of Salesforce, with the deep, native integration available between the two systems, you can achieve incredible sales results.

When pricing your Call Center in a Hubspot+Salesforce technical environment, you have to take into consideration:

- Number of Inbound Leads Being Generated Daily
- Number of API Calls this requires to and from Salesforce
- Number of Salesforce Users, they usually price by seat

---

90.   Call Center can refer to a central geographic place where many people work, or it can be completely virtualized.

- Other Software required to make your Call Center Work
- Call Center Phone Software, such as Five9, and the number of required phone numbers
- The space required for your people to work in
- The equipment – high quality headsets are a must
- Training

It is very easy to set this type of environment up these days and you can literally start with one person. This is drastically different, re: cheaper than the days where it would cost a minimum of $200,000 just for the hardware for a true, interactive, voice response system. This is not to say the cost won't be substantial and the cost will rise over time. Count on it.

Your biggest challenge will be staffing your call center or if you outsource, ensuring your call center has sufficient surge capacity to support you in peak load times.

But the absolutely critical aspect to getting it to work is having and continuously improving your call scripts. Otherwise, no one is benefitting from what has already been learned about what works and what doesn't.

What is a Call Center?

A Call center can be anything from a one-man shop calling his customers to an actual call center with hundreds of call center personnel spread across multiple time zones connected via what is called a VOIP or Voice Over Internet Protocol system. Hubspot mostly functions as an outbound call center platform while several partner products turn it into a full outbound call center.

Salesforce

For many businesses, Salesforce will be the Call Center system in use. Fortunately, it integrates natively into Hubspot. That means it uses an API key to connect the two systems and then you can adjust the settings within Hubspot to reflect how you want to handle data coming from and going to Salesforce. What is a little tricky is deciding which system should be the system of record. The conceptual data models of Hubspot and Salesforce are different. Salesforce uses an Account and Opportunity approach, whereas Hubspot starts with the contact record, then sells (does a deal).

In other scenarios, you may have a CPQ (Configure, Price and Quote) system, such as Zuora, integrated into Salesforce, which means Zuora is the 'deal maker' and product catalog home of record. It is also possible that there may be a Call Center dialing software, such as Five9 integrated into Hubspot. We've also seen various solutions that help keep track of television advertising driven inbound calls, i.e., Callrail. Each of these systems will generate some sort of activity record both within Salesforce as well as within Hubspot.

For the marketer, this means there is a lot more information to deal with, specifically to segment on. But it also means the marketer and everybody else in the organization has to know a lot more about the data models of the connected systems.

That activity data in Salesforce is also of great value to the Call Center personnel. With it, they can pull up the customer's complete activity record while on the call with a customer. When you get a call from someone, say a recruiter, who is probably working from a call center, and they start asking you for information you've already supplied, it means they don't have this capability.

Marketing can and should be looking at how the information in Salesforce is being used throughout the sales process. That way, they can help ensure the sales team has the latest information and as well, make sure more of the sales team's time is spent selling, not developing content. It is also a great way to uncover the best content from a performance standpoint.

CHAPTER FIVE

FREE TRIAL

For almost all of our Hubspot Inbound Marketing customers, we start with the 30 day free trial. It provides many valuable benefits, such as visibility into your actual website visitors. It is during the Free Trial that we are able to gather the required sizing information.

We've already discussed the process for sizing. There are only a few key questions that must be answered to arrive at a proper sizing proposal for your marketing platform:

◆ Total number of email contacts
◆ Total number of primary domains (URLs)
◆ Current website traffic

To size your Hubspot Sales System, it is somewhat easier:

◆ Total number of sales people

◆ Contacts (the free version includes up to 1,000,000 contacts)

There are a few add-ons that you may need if you're just a Hubspot Sales System user, but not many. They include the CMS, Reports Ad-On and API Ad-On (only required for very high volume sales organizations.

You Need to Know Your System Landscape

It should be clear to you by now that your business is going to be or is a system of systems. That's why we recommend you start out your Hubspot sizing exercising by developing a system landscape diagram. You may find you either have systems that can be integrated into Hubspot, like Salesforce or Five9, or you may recognize you have system gaps that will need to be filled by an application. It is often the case that these systems need you to have a certain level of Hubspot available if they are to be integrated.

Pricing the System is Sizing and Volume Driven

Hubspot has a fairly simple pricing system, all of which is available on their website. Some businesses can and do just go online, select their package and buy it. In the vast majority of cases, you will need to work with a Hubspot partner to get your pricing. It's a simple, pain free process.

The reason for working with Hubspot partner is very clear - Hubspot doesn't provide Inbound Marketing services. They have a methodology that all partners follow, which means when a partner, such as ourselves, request a payment link, our Hubspot Channel Account Manager ask us a series of qualification questions about our potential customers. They don't want to sell their software to a business for whom it is not a good fit. That's why they rely on partners' who know their software and the partners particular niche.

You May Be a Good Fit or Not

If you've gotten this far and know that your product or service is a considered sale, then you need to know that during the trial, there's one other element of your business that will need to be evaluated. Do you have a marketing funnel? If not, how likely, in terms of required change management, are you likely to be able and willing to work with a partner to create one?

It Comes Down to Story

By story, we mean the story of your business and what it sells. Why does it exist. What's the motivation beyond what it is you do. The more clearly defined this story is, the easier it will be to see whether Hubspot Inbound Marketing is the right approach or some other approach would be better for you.

Your story also comes into play when evaluating whether you're a good fit for Hubspot using other criteria that are well established. For instance, if you're product or service is fairly low-cost, say below $500, then it generally won't work to market it using Inbound Marketing.

Another aspect of your story is how you sell. If you sell directly to customers, which would normally be a good fit, versus indirectly, through channels, which will not be a good fit. On the other hand, there are many sales approaches where different channels are blended, and it may make sense to approach sales from an Inbound way.

What You Have Versus What You Need

During your free trial, you'll be highly encouraged to start and if at all possible, complete your content audit. Here's what you will find in most cases. You will have content of all types and of all quality, or not much at all. We highly recommend you keep track of your audit results using a tool like our content audit tool.

The second part of the content budgeting process is mapping your existing content to your marketing and sales funnel stages. You will find that you have some content for some parts, and none for other parts. Even if you find that your existing content is not 'marketing ready', go ahead and map it to the funnel stage where it belongs. That way, you can estimate the level of effort it will take to transform it into what you need.

Where you see empty spots in your content map, you will need to follow our content ideation process. This requires combining your knowledge of your buyer persona, researching keywords and concepts and then a good deal of directed imagination to at least generate content titles. A good rule of thumb for content to support your marketing funnel is 5, 3, 1. This means have 5 Top of Funnel (TOFU), 3 Middle of Funnel (MOFU), and 1 Bottom of Funnel (BOFU) offers. Don't worry if you don't have this exact quantity, just know you need enough to fill the funnel and pull your prospects through the funnel.

Our site, despite our small size, has over 400 content offers on it, which we created based on our own expertise. It didn't happen overnight, nor will yours. That's why they say Inbound Marketing is the long game, meaning it will take six months to see results. But your results act like compound interest. Each piece of highly optimized content accumulates SEO credit (we call it Google Juice) over time.

There are a lot of different content types you can develop, including ebooks, white-papers, checklist, podcasts, videos, blogs, quizzes, calculators and product selectors. Though it is possible to develop calculators and product selectors totally within Hubspot, you should know there are a large number software providers that provide even more functionality. The bigger issue you're facing is that customers expect interactivity. This requires not just tools, but imagination.

Though we don't want to provide any hard and fast prices for any type of content, you should probably budget around 3 to 5 thousand for a basic 10 page high quality, Subject Matter Expert, white paper. If you have internal resources, you expect it to take about 3 days to plan, develop, write and publish a complete campaign, including, forms, landing pages, blogs, smart list, workflows, and lead nurturing emails.

For interactive content, it goes on up from there, while Sales Tools, also a key content deliverable, can cost from 50 thousand to 500 thousand dollars. We've been collecting sample calculator URLs for inspiration, and you can find a small sample list in the footnotes to this chapter.[91]

Though we produced our own content, we still wanted to know what it would cost to have it done. Using sites like Zerys, Expresswriters, medially, SnapApp, Ceros and others, we were able to estimate that our content has taken about $914,000 in Senior SAP consulting and developer time. It has paid for itself many times over, and keeps generating leads day-after-day. For very large firms, this is not a major expenditure, considering that many TV commercials run from 300 to 500k and well beyond that, just in production cost. The key thing to keep in mind is that you don't need to have this much budget on day one of your project, indeed,

---

[91.]   https://www.mapr.com/resources/hadoop-total-cost-of-ownership-calculator

http://www.dinkytown.net/

http://valueofalike.com/

https://www.impactbnd.com/expected-roi-of-inbound-marketing

http://www.reshorenow.org/TCO_Estimator.cfm

https://miniwebtool.com/

https://offers.Hubspot.com/thank-you/freelance-hourly-rate-calculator?inc-salary=250000&inc-work-days=4&inc-work-hours=8&inc-vacation-days=15&inc-sick-days=5&inc-holidays=30&inc-billable-rate=65&exp-office-space=200&exp-web-hosting=200&exp-internet=840&exp-pm-tools=960&exp-mkt-software=2400&exp-ad-spend=5000&exp-acct-software=360&exp-acct-fees=600&exp-medical=1800&exp-travel=5000&exp-tech=2000&exp-retirement=11000&exp-taxes=6000&exp-miscellaneous=500

https://www.Hubspot.com/ads-calculator?ads-budget=2000&cpc=2.50&conversion-rate=3.00&average-price=2500&ltc=10

https://www.business.qld.gov.au/running-business/finances-cash-flow/managing-money/break-even-point

for most small firms, this is outside the scope of possibilities. You will need this over time. A good rule of thumb is to plan on it taking about 3 weeks end-to-end to truly launch a campaign. That's what Hubspot, with their in-house content factory, have stated it takes them.

For companies in deeply technical, highly competitive markets, i.e., SAP implementation partners, SAP Consultants joined up with content writers is going to be the only viable solution. Why is that? Because SAP has an Industry Solution Go-to-Market strategy. The SAP consultants who know what makes SAP special for a particular industry, such as Retail or Aerospace & Defense, are expensive, always booked, and probably not great at writing marketing ready material. That's why you need trained journalist available. To get the story and turn it into something that sells.

Have a Content Plan or Don't Do This

Here's the bottom line on budgeting for content. Have a content plan, budget for it, build it. Our successful customers have one thing in common - a content plan which drove the Inbound Marketing effort. Our customers who did not succeed did not have a content plan.

We've Got an Hour

During your free trial, we always start with a one-hour free consultation. What do we do during that hour? To start with, and if it makes sense for your business type, we're going to set you up with a free trial, which is good for 30 days. What does 'set you up' mean though?

We will create a Hubspot Portal (your instance of Hubspot) which will provide us what is called the Hubspot tracking code. It's a piece of magic. We'll ask you to insert it on your website, or if possible, we will do it for you (takes a minute if it is a typical Wordpress Website or similar system). It will begin to track your website traffic.

What benefit is that to you?

For starters, it will tell you whether you have any website traffic, and if so, how much. During the FREE Trial period, (beyond if you purchase the system), it will also tell you which channels your traffic is coming from. These channels include: Organic, Direct, Social, Paid Ads, Paid Social and Referrals and possibly a few others. The code also listens to any 'conversions' happening on your website, and captures those contacts into your contact database. Now you know what is actually driving conversions on your website, if any are happening.[92]

You may have Google Analytics installed on your site if there is any traffic, you will now be able to see a lot of valuable information that Google Analytics does not show. This is not to say that Google Analytics doesn't provide valuable information - it does. But it is increasingly encrypting what you need to know to provide a better user experience due to all the regulations[93] being imposed by various government entities around the world, especially in Europe.

[92.] In many, if not most cases, no conversions are happening, unfortunately.

[93.] The European Union's GDPR regulation being among the most stringent of these new regulations.

With the technical issues out of the way, we'll start to discuss your goals[94], such as annual revenue goals, and your current marketing and sales approach. We'll also start collecting the information we need to size and price your system, such as contacts. It is very likely you won't have this number handy, but you'll come away from the meeting with a list of to-do's which include finding out this number and probably cleaning up the contact information you do have.

Finally, this is your time to ask questions and start to learn about the Inbound Marketing and Inbound Sales Methodology. If you're really curious, we'll show where to start doing some actual online training. Hint: Your Hubspot Portal.

What to Expect in a Marketing Proposal

Up to this point, we've been collecting a lot of information regarding goals, content, timelines, and contacts. We've also tried to get a deeper understanding of your sales process. Next you will receive a customized proposal that lays out the What, Who, Why, and How of an Inbound Marketing project.

We're almost set. But first, a few preliminary decisions will need to be made before we begin. Will we be moving you fully onto Hubspot? Or will we keep some or all of your website on the existing web platform? In just about every case, our recommendation is going to be to migrate your entire website to Hubspot. This is really the only way to get the full benefit[95] of the platform in our experience. You should know that some

---

94. If you have no annual revenue goals, making this work will be more than a little challenging.
95. Chief among the full benefits you won't be able to enjoy will be use of the full contextual marketing capabilities of the Hubspot system.

companies buy Hubspot just for the analytics! Others host only their blog on the platform, while others only do landing pages. For our purposes, let's just go with the Big Bang, 100% migration to Hubspot.

You Get a Migration Assessment

The first thing that must happen for the Big Bang migration is for the Hubspot migration team to do an assessment of your website. Shortly afterwards, they will provide you with the assessment results for your signature. For the most part, most things can be migrated as is, but somethings cannot be migrated. They keep increasing the number and variety of widgets they can migrate, but keep in mind, they are also looking to get you a platform optimized for lead generation and in many cases, those little bells and whistles don't really help the cause much. Very complex web items, like existing calculators will not generally be migratable. But they can be recreated using what are called Hubspot custom modules[96].

Gearing Up the Migration Team

Once the migration team has received the sign-off and you have signed up for your Hubspot account, the migration team will need from 7 to 21 days to complete the migration. What does 'complete' mean. The migration team will recreate each page of your website to basically look and feel just like the current site.

[96.] Hubspot has its own language, Hubl, which allows you to do some very sophisticated programming.

In addition to recreating your website, they will also create templates for you to use. It is very important that you know what templates they are obligated to produce per their contract and that you verify that they are there.

As your Hubspot implementation partner, we will be in frequent contact with the migration team. Part of our quality assurance process is to test and validate every single item the migration team produces, including doing a page-by-page comparison between your existing site and the new Hubspot site. Our Go-Live checks typically take around two weeks, and slightly longer if any identified issues have to be fixed by the migration team.

The Hubspot migration is a hugely important part of getting you live on the Hubspot system. It is also a valuable service which it is wise to take full advantage of. That's why we call it out in particular as a 'special interest' item to pay attention to. We have good and not so good experiences with it, and today, we would have to say that we are a difficult task master for Hubspot (working on behalf of our clients) when it comes to migrations. Trust us, you will thank us for this.

Go Over It With a Fine-Tooth Comb

Though we have great confidence and trust in the migration team, we have found that you need about two weeks to do a formal acceptance test of your migrated website. Why so long? Because you need to go over every single page with a fine-tooth comb. If there were spelling or grammar mistakes in your old site, they got migrated. Now's a great time to fix them.

You also need to create a live page from each and every one of your migrated templates. These templates are key to your future Inbound Marketing success. The migration team is usually very responsive to correcting issues you find, as long as it is within the acceptance test window, which is about two weeks. We also highly recommend you test every form on the website. By test, we mean take a look at it and make sure it says what it should say, and as well, submit your information and make sure it is working.

Finally, you need to test your email templates. You need to test both the automated and simple response templates. It is here where you really, really, really need to dig in deep into the system. The email testing tool allows you to test across a wide range of mobile devices. Test every one of them. We've never received a cleanly migrated system that didn't need extensive work with the CSS code to make the email templates 'production ready'.

Once you've tested every element of your migrated website, you're now ready to go live. This has gotten progressively easier over the years, to the point where in many cases, it is a single press of the button type of affair, especially if your domain provider is a major provider like Godaddy. For most domain providers, Hubspot provides detailed, step-by-step instructions on taking your site live. Just know this. There will need to be fairly complex CNAME changes made. Where it may get hairy is if your site is being run by a smaller player, i.e., a small server in a small garage[97]. This is generally much more complicated to make happen, but we've done it many times and always got the system live.

[97.]   One of our South American clients literally had a 'friend' whose setup consisted of a webserver in his garage.

You're Live, Now What?

Live means it is time to retest, and then retest some more. If you've taken the proper amount of care with the post migration inspection, then this should be a breeze. It will still take some time, though. Again, be thorough here. Test every form by submitting it. Read every page using the skills of a proof reader[98] in a newspaper. If you run across issues, do a screen cam of it. Don't skip it and think you'll get back to it. You won't, but your customers will. Now you can start building out your inbound marketing offers!

Let's Make Some Sales

Going live with sales should be approached with as much attention to detail as the going live with marketing required. The Hubspot Sales/CRM is a very easy piece of software to use and to set up. That said, the go-live can vary greatly depending on the type of product or service you sell as well as the size of the sales team and sales process maturity.

During your Sales Go-Live, we'll need to identify everybody who needs a Hubspot Sales Log-On, as well as their role. The system allows you to define a fairly granular level of access, and we have found that most sales managers still like to keep a fairly tight hold on who sees what. We will also help you identify stages in your Sales Pipeline and model them in the system. We will also need to create the first series of Sales E-Mail templates and, if appropriate, set them up in the Sales Workflow tool, called Sequences. Finally, we'll need to connect up your phones[99] to the system.

---

98. Newspaper proof readers had a special mark up language they used - you just need a red pen and attention to detail
99. The system uses VOIP and you can connect your iPhone device as well as many other calling solutions.

Along with your email templates, we'll need to set up your meetings tool, which uses Google Calendar and Hubspot. We also highly recommend you create a common corporate wide signature block, using the Hubspot signature generator. You must ensure that everybody uses the standard company signature on all of their email clients, including their mobile phone. One of the easiest ways to destroy sales productivity is to make it hard for your customers to find you because they can't find your contact details in your emails. Believe us, that's where everyone is looking.

It is also during this time that we teach you about the various contact and company data fields you see in the system, and define any new ones, such as calculated fields, you may need. During this time, we will also set up workflows that automate some of the more mundane sales tasks, like setting up a deal with a defined value when someone converts on the website on a pricing page or views a certain page, like a contact us page. This particular set up task requires on-going fine tuning. The system can quickly create an overwhelming number of deals or tasks, which just leads to user frustration and low close rates.

We'll also set up your on-site chat and chat bot. This means you'll have to man this system and also decide who and how you will interact with known contacts. The chat bot has complex capabilities and provides a conversational modeling capability that can be very useful to segment visitors, among many uses.

Setting Up the Sales KPIs

The system comes with both standard reports and a reports add-on, which provides extensive customizable reports development capability. Here's what you should track to start with.

My Top 4:

- Deals Closed
- Closed Amount/by product/service/rep/territory vs. Goal
- Number of Calls Worked Per Day/Hour vs. Goal
- Number of Calls Worked within Five Minutes vs. Goal

My Top All the Rest

- Total Pipeline Value vs. Goal
- Deals per Pipeline Stage vs. Goal
- E-Mails Sent/Open vs. Goal
- Sales Content Used and Provided/Touched by Marketing

Sales is More Than Systems

In my role as Industry Principal for SAP, I found that though the systems are important, the one-on-one sales mentoring I delivered to my account executives was critical to hitting my numbers. It is no different with any of my customers. Go-Live is not a one and done affair. It requires both the setting up and training on the system. Once that part is done, then it usually requires Sales Coaching. Though there are a lot of different Sales Strategies, I have found that successful sales people have to get a few common things right:

- Product knowledge
- Communication ability, both written and oral
- Proposals that take the friction out of the process.

The first pre-requisite, Hubspot cannot fix. It has to come from product training and experience, yet a sales person doesn't typically get too much of either to start with. It means the key to success is on-going self-directed training.

The second pre-requisite is also a non-Hubspot or really, a non-system issue. A top salesman needs to practice communicating. Of course, there are plenty of communication courses you can take, but it is a basic prerequisite to be able to write clearly and speak clearly, both one-on-one or in a group situation. One great way to improve your skills is to join a local theater. I advised many members of my SAP pre-sales teams that they should consider joining. Toastmasters is also a good option. But nothing beats doing it, day-after-day, in front of a crowd. If the sales process is on the phone, the same holds true. Nothing beats doing it, day-after-day. The big difference is usually the availability of sales scripts and recordings which can then be used to improve the scripts.

The last and what I've come to appreciate as the critical piece of the puzzle, is mastering the proposal process. In my previous jobs, proposals were and still are, long, tedious, detailed documents. By long, think 200 pages and up. This was necessary due to the complex RFPs we were responding to as well as the complexity of our solutions. What our proposals were not was easily signed. In today's market, the move toward CPQ systems (Configure, Price and Quote), makes assembling a proposal much more efficient, and more effective. For instance, in our own business, we use a system called Pandadoc, which allows us to provide a rich media experience, along with a payment mechanism. This is fully integrated into Hubspot and has saved us a lot of time as well as allowing us to increase the number of proposals we get out the door. In fact, we have largely turned the Professional Services business into an e-commerce business, a long standing goal of mine!

CPQ Means You Know What You're Selling

If you've read this far, you know that one of the major problems every business faces is knowing what they are selling. When you use a CPQ system, you quickly realize you have to know this. If you've ever tried to create a catalog, whether for products or services, you know that it requires clear thinking. It is here, in the catalog creation process, that you will need to determine the specifics of each offer. This can grow very complex, very quickly.

One of the biggest challenges for your sales team is knowing what is meant by any particular item in your product catalog. There may be hierarchical tree structures buried within your catalog. What you're offering may have changed over time while the actual catalog entry remains static (but it can be edited). The challenge is creating something that can be reused, understood by everyone, and quickly used to create a proposal.

While most 'internet marketing' gurus will tell you focus is the key, you may well find your offerings are broad because your actual business is complex. For example, setting up a new e-commerce business from scratch[100] and connecting the plumbing is no small undertaking.

Rare Combination of Skills

Learning Inbound Marketing is both simple and complex, all at the same time. It requires advanced skills with a computer, but not computer scientist level. It also requires the ability to write clearly. I've hired and trained several of them myself, and of course, learned the skill myself. The training available from Hubspot[101] on the Inbound Marketing methodology provides you with essentially a master's degree in Inbound Marketing and the Inbound Sales training is excellent as well. I've taken and passed all of their certifications every year for the past 8 years.

There is a also a huge role for developers. If you come up with a calculator or product selector or other advanced use case of the Hubspot system, you're probably going to need a developer. We've now built at least 17 calculators and online tools, as of the writing of this book in 2019. What has worked is for me to first to develop the calculator I have in mind in Excel, and once that is working, and as simply as possible, then I turn it over to my brother, who is a hard core Hubspot developer. He can usually turn them around in a few days. The more advanced tools we've come up with, for instance, an online version of the Hubspot Inbound Marketing Assessment tool, requires considerably more 'tricks of the trade' than creating a calculator.

[100.] We've now done this enough times for our Shopify e-commerce practice to say we have it down pat, but every business is unique.

[101.] Both from the Hubspot Academy as well as onsite Hubspot training events.

It requires knowing how to intelligently use the list tool, the design templates[102] we've developed and some coding, to get it all to work. We've seen many other tools people have developed as well, so you also need a lot of imagination to make this work. But working technically isn't the goal. Making it work to generate leads and ultimately, sales, is the goal. That's where you need very advanced knowledge of Hubspot and the particular business you're developing the solution for.

You Can Learn the Hubspot Tool in Two Weeks

The tool can easily be mastered in a couple of weeks if you work on it all day, every day, under the tutelage of an expert user. I know, I've trained my own hires up in about that much time. That gets them tolerably dangerous. To get to a level where you can demonstrate leadership, you will need considerably more time. I would say that six months minimum is a good figure to get to where you can trust someone to dream up, develop, create, publish, test, test, test, measure and improve an offer. In other words, the challenge is not the tool. The tool is exceptionally well designed, backed up with world class support and comes with always improving training.

We Start to Build Your Inbound Team During the Trial

As you can tell, someone who masters Inbound Marketing is going to be a rare find. During the trial, we usually spend quite a bit of time helping our clients identify who will be on the Inbound Marketing team. In those cases where they want to completely outsource it to us, we of course, will take that on. However,

---

102.   Our proprietary design templates are critical to building these complex tools for our clients.

for the best results, our goal is to get our clients set up to do Inbound Marketing with their own internal resources. In the past, when it came to internet marketing, which isn't really a defined methodology, it was not unusual to see the work off-shored. Your ideal Inbound Marketing team and team member knows your business inside out. This requires constant interaction with the business. You'll be investing in them in terms of providing them tools, time to learn and getting under the sheets of your business.

In reality, by the end of the trial, it will be clear you don't have enough resources. But at least now, we can build a plan to get you the resources you need, get them trained, and figure out how you're going to hold on to them. The marketer labor market has a high degree of turn-over. Most businesses that are struggling to make their sales number are still treating marketing like a commodity. How low can you go is the operative mind set. This simply won't work, if it ever did.

On the other hand, if you're using a leading edge, highly regarded system like Hubspot, marketers will want to work with you. Even if they graduated from university yesterday, they probably have only heard of Hubspot, but will not have had the chance to work with the tool.

Finally, know this. A World Class Inbound Marketer can make or break your company. They are the lever you're looking for.

It's Go Time

During the 30-day free trial, we will have set up at least one offer[103] on your site, regardless of whether you have any traffic or not. Our goal is to see if you have an offer than can be turned into a sale during that time. For long, complex sales cycles, such as those required to sell SAP, no sale will have been made. It usually takes many months to close these deals. However, if you get a lead in via an offer we put up, you have a very clear idea that this will work for you.

By the end of the trial period, we will have already decided if you're a good fit for Hubspot and whether we're a good fit for you. If so, we'll make our proposal, as will Hubspot (their subscription must be signed via them), and your migration will kick-off. Somewhere between 7 and 21 days later, they'll release the system for acceptance.

The actual go-live requires some settings to be made in your CNAME panel in your domain name provider, usually someone like Godaddy.

---

103. This is usually going to be by using a simple landing page and Hubspot form to convert traffic into leads. This is often not something a business has been able to do before.

Inbound For All

The basic Inbound Marketing training course is available to the public on www.Hubspot.com. The remaining, extensive training, is available to subscribers[104]. During the trial, whoever from your team is going to be your Inbound Marketer, will be asked to at least complete the basic Inbound Methodology training.

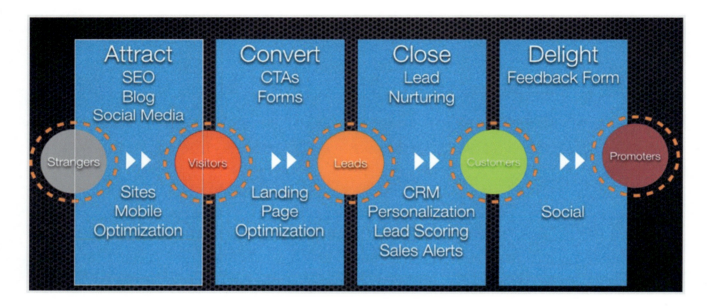

The Hidden Secret to the Hubspot Training

Our minimum Inbound Marketing engagement is six months, while one year is recommended. Six months is about how long it usually takes to start seeing any results. Here's the little secret we are sharing with you

---

[104.] Subscribers refers to customers who have purchased a Hubspot subscription, at any level.

for the first time ever. Our implementation will follow the sequence of events in the Hubspot Inbound Marketing training! That's why we'll be 'strongly recommending' you complete the next training module each week. For instance, there's a module on creating your buyer persona. Lo and behold, there's a point in the implementation when we focus on creating your buyer personas. Time to create your content plan? That's why we asked everyone on the team to have completed that module prior to the meeting.

<u>Marketing</u>

Is Social Media Going to Work For You?

It's very rare these days for a business to not have at least a presence on social media. The primary social media channels[105] include: Facebook, Instagram, YouTube, LinkedIn, Pinterest and Twitter. During your trial, we'll connect up Hubspot to your channels, and start collecting data. It's also possible to publish to these channels, even during your trial. Each channel is for specific types of audiences, and your audience needs to be identified.

If you don't currently have a presence on a particular Social Media channel, we'll help you get that set up. We'll most likely have to work with you closely to develop a Social Media marketing strategy as well, regardless of where you currently are at social media wise.

---

[105]. These are the primary ones as of the time of the writing of this book. It's very likely there will be new ones, while some of these may fade to irrelevance or get bought out or combined, as has happened many times since the Internet Revolution began.

Looking for Low Hanging Fruit

At this point in my Inbound Marketing career, I've personally done enough SEO work that many people think I am a magician. I am not. I just keep studying whatever Google says, and then look for the easiest things to fix, commonly called low hanging fruit.

SEO or Search Engine Optimization is neither purely a technical exercise nor a purely functional exercise. It, like almost everything else about Inbound Marketing requires knowledge of how the tools work, what the business is selling and a great deal of research. We'll set up your Google Analytics[106] account during the trial phase, and let it start gathering information. Keep in mind, we'll be limited to the free Google Analytics tool. Google offers a high-end paid version of the tool, and if you're a candidate for this tool, we'll work with you to deploy it as well. There are, in fact, many other tools you might use. The most important one, of course, is from Hubspot. During the free trial, you'll actually have access to the enterprise version of the tool, meaning you will be able to do everything an enterprise customer can do.

Getting Your Hubspot Tracking Code Setup

One of the very first steps to successfully run a Hubspot trial is installing your Hubspot tracking code. It's a very small piece of code, once installed, you usually never have to touch it again, unlike Google Analytics, Google Adwords or Facebook, all of which require near constant tweaking.

---

106.   If you're one of our larger customers, you may have a paid Google tool we will use.

Here's What It Will Tell You

One of the most useful pieces of information it provides comes from the sources report. This shows the traffic, by, you guessed it, the various sources. You might say, so what, so does Google Analytics. True, but the Hubspot sources tool tells you how many contacts each traffic source generated and how many customers each traffic source generated. After you're all set up and generating a steady flow of customers, it will also tell you how long it takes to convert a lead into a customer, by channel. Google won't do that. In fact, over the years, Google has consistently reduced the amount of information it provides, including, critically, keyword information.

There's a new superhero on the SEO block though. That is the Google Search Console integration to Hubspot. At first, I didn't see much useful information coming in from this. But now, I do. What does it do? It tells me what search terms people were using when Google decided to show one of my pages. It also tells me how many clicks the specific page received, how many times Google decided to show it (known as impressions) and the Clickthrough Rate in Percentage. So what, you say. Well, now that you know what Google actually thinks your page is about and whether or not it did good job of matching up user's search intent to it, you can use the search terms they used to upgrade the page or just create a brand new one around an attractive looking term.

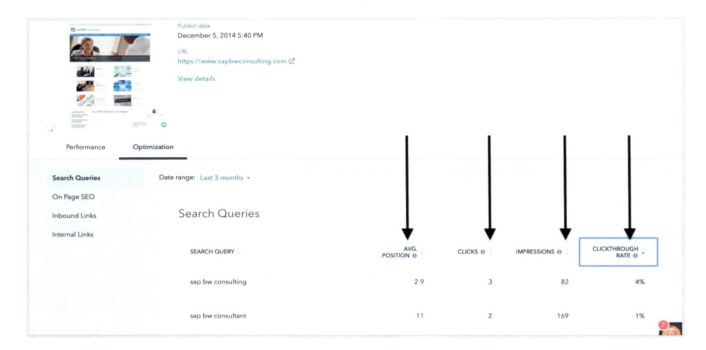

There is More SEO Goodness Buried Here

When you combine this information with the concept of Pillar Pages, wherein you have one deep page of information for a particular subject, i.e., your service or product offering, with the Google search term information, the Hubspot optimizer really starts to shine. You won't see much during the free trail, but once you build out your site, with one or more pillar pages, you get recommendations that are amazing. It will literally start telling you specific, contextually relevant phrases to include in your page.

What it translates into is you have a system that provides actionable information for you to continuously optimize your website with. This is one of the major differentiators between Hubspot and trying to do all this on a Wordpress site. We've seen about a 20% improvement in website traffic and daily conversions since we set up this integration.

Content Strategy First

I've previously told you how important it is to do a content audit. During your free trial, you'll be trying to learn a lot about the system, the Inbound Marketing methodology and the Inbound Sales methodology. All of your activity will ultimately be fueled by content. Therefore, having a content strategy is one of the most critical development task of your Inbound Marketing journey.

What is a Content Strategy? Here's how I define it. It is the creation of a comprehensive content plan that supports every step of your business. It will define the messaging your customer encounters from their first encounter with your business all the way through to the post purchase experience and beyond. A truly comprehensive content strategy will include not just marketing, but sales and service as well. This is one area where marketing needs to lead, and everybody else needs to follow.

Content Plan

Once you have your content strategy in place and your content audit done, next comes the research phase. This involves doing keyword research using tools such as Google Keyword Planner and SEMRush. Ubërsuggest is another excellent tool. If they exist, then customer questions are an excellent source of content ideas. When you're done with your research, it is time to produce your content ideas. Fortunately, the Inbound Marketing methodology has evolved enough that now there is a sort of roadmap to follow when initiating the ideation phase of your content planning.

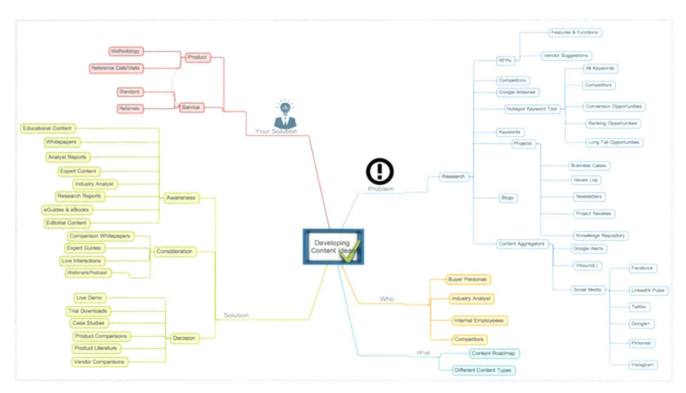

Content Planning Mind Map

If you're doing it right, you should end up with a content plan with different types of content that fit into each phase of the Inbound Marketing methodology. Here's a template you can use to slot in your content ideas.

Buyer Stages	Awareness	Consideration	Decision
User Behavior	Have realized and expressed symptoms of a potential problem or opportuntiy	Have clearly defined and given a name to their problem or opportunity	Have defined their solution strategy, method or approach
Research & Info Needs	Research focused on vendor neutral 3ʳᵈ party information around identifying problems or symptoms	Committed to researching and understanding all of the available approaches/methods to solving their defined problem or opportunity	Researching supporting documentation, data, benchmarks or endorsements to make or recommend a final decision
Content Types	• Analyst reports • Research Reports • eGuides & eBooks • Editorial Content • Expert Content • White Papers • Educational Content	• Comparison white papers • Expert Guides • Live Interactions • Webcast/Podcast/Video	• Vendor Comparisons • Product Comparisons • Case Studies • Trial Download • Product Literature • Live Demo
Key Terms	Troubleshoot / Issue / Resolve / Risks — Upgrade / Improve / Optimize / Prevent	Solution / Provider / Service / Supplier — Tool / Device / Software / Appliance	Compare / Vs. / Versus / Comparison — Pros and Cons / Benchmarks / Review / Test
Example	Users Haven't Accepted My BI Systems. What's wrong?	My BW System is Also Slow. How Can I improve Performance	I can upgrade it, I can Implement Dashboard Best Practices. Each Cost 250k but the Upgrade takes longer

For each of our clients, we use this same template to create their content plan. We recommend you combine Buyer Persona, Problem and Keyword to develop your working title for each piece of content.

How Much is Enough

Though I can't give you a hard and fast rule, here's a rule of thumb or two to follow. First, keep this relationship in mind: For each piece of downloadable content, you'll need at least one Blog, one landing page and one thank you page. In addition, you will need a Call-to-Action or CTA. Generally speaking, you will need about 60 blogs to see solid traction, and about 200 to be seen as a reference site by Google and others. That means 60 pieces of downloadable content to 200 pieces of downloadable content. That's a major undertaking and cannot be produced overnight. All of this content will need to be connected via a series of behavioral based lead nurturing emails.

How Should I Sequence My Content Production

Remember, TOFU, MOFU, BOFU? Top of the funnel, middle of the funnel, bottom of the funnel? That's how I would build my content. But in reverse. I always start by building out the BOFU offer first, then working my way up the funnel. This makes it considerably more difficult but far more effective to develop the content plan. But if you want to sell, this goes along with knowing what you sell and knowing how you sell it.

How Should I Manage This Content Production Line

It's very easy these days to work as a team when producing this content. I like to set up a shared Google Drive (others use Dropbox). Whenever I am kicking off a project, I set up a series of folders I have found are required on all projects. One of those is Content Plan, the other is Offers. A third critical folder is Buyer

Persona. With that in place, and everyone on both the customer and our side in place, I make sure everyone knows how to install the Google Drive onto their hard-drive. The challenge here is to only keep a local copy of the documents/folders when needed. Otherwise, people will complain that google is eating their hard drive. Any third party content providers should also have access to this set of folders. They will also want to review the buyer persona worksheet.

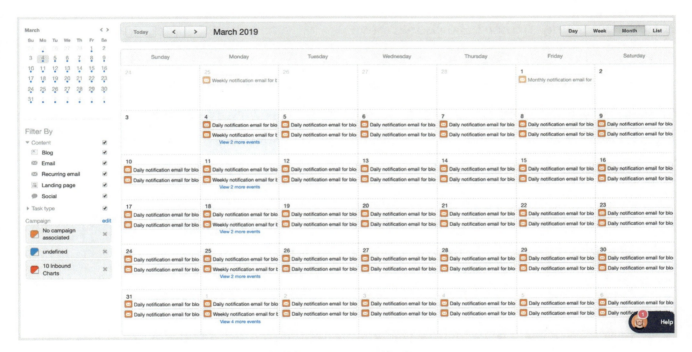

Hubspot Content Calendar

Though you could use many different approaches to keeping track of your content production line, I recommend just using the Hubspot Calendar. It allows you to assign work within the Hubspot system, and filter and sort in any number of ways. I have tried using various other solutions, such as Google Calendar, Outlook, or iCal. They all work great for what they were designed for, which wasn't managing a content production pipeline. Whenever I've had the luxury of a large team[107] of content producers, including bloggers, social media team, copywriters, graphic artist and SEO experts, this was the only tool that really worked for me. I recommend you learn from my experience.

CRM System Setup

If Only We Could Predict Who Would Buy

Actually, we can. Within Hubspot, there is both an automated and manual predictive lead scoring[108] system. Of course, to make them work, you need sales! That's why it's a good idea to use Hubspot CRM. If you can make your sale using the Hubspot platform, then the system can make predictions with little intervention on your part.

If you have enough lead data and sales data, with definitions in place for Marketing Qualified Leads (MQLs) and Sales Qualified Leads (SQLs), then you can use the predicted lead scoring to guide the sales team to the hottest leads.

If you don't have enough sales volume or you want to tweak the predicted lead scores, you make manual adjustments to the tool. This is why it is absolutely critical that the sales team use the system to make sales and that they record all the activity in the system. From hard won experience, I can tell you that the vast

---

[107]. By large, I mean we had 13 members in-house working on pure Hubspot related tasks, including blogging, content creation and people assigned to a single social media channel. We also had contractors, and used the facilities of outside organizations, such as studios. Many teams are much larger than this and Hubspot allows you to create teams to support large organizations.

[108]. This is one of the more powerful ways to segment your contact database, and usually the most profitable. https://www.youtube.com/watch?v=bswihdH_ybM

majority of data in your CRM is put there long after the deal is closed. As you can imagine, this invalidates the statistics and must be managed to be avoided. The system really shines in this area. It was designed to make data entry largely a non-event for the sales person. They just make their phone calls, send their emails and otherwise do what they do to make the sale.

Predictive Lead Scoring and E-Mail

E-Commerce uses e-mail for a variety of reasons, particularly abandoned shopping cart recovery and for lead nurturing. By combining predictive lead scoring with your e-commerce email segmentation strategy, you can focus your message delivery to the exact person at the exact time to achieve maximum sales efficiency.

What Should Go In My Sales Pipeline?

If you've followed the Inbound Sales training, you've already ran across the answer - the least amount of sales stages possible. The basic rule to follow is to only put in pipeline stages that require activity on the part of the customer. The pipeline stages that require action on the part of you, the vendor, are better handled with Tasks. If you follow this concept, then you should end up with a fairly simple, and thus, manageable sales pipeline. I've seen an 18 step pipeline that actually was correct. But it tended to spin off a never ending supply of excel sheets as the boss tried to discern what was happening with the deals. Worked, but not well.

One Exception

Within the Professional Services world, i.e., SAP consulting, we have an initiating stage, which we have seen called various different names, but usually goes something like this - Ops Identified & Initial Contact. There is no customer action in this stage, but it does tell you where something is afoot.

Use the Force

Your sales pipeline uses a concept called probability weighted pipeline. It simply means that a deal at a certain stage has a probability of closing of X. Here's why it's sort of a big deal. Quick war story. In my previous role, I had an annual Sales Quota of $4,500,000 for net new license sales. I had a number of metrics I needed to keep in mind when managing my pipeline, one of the most important was my pipeline coverage. In short, I needed to have 3X pipeline coverage (initially it was 2.5X) in my sales pipeline. Doing the math, that meant that I needed to have $4,5000,000 * 3 = $13,500,000 in my pipe at any one time. You should know that I typically exceeded quota by 500% which meant my year-end bonus was 5X. In order to do that, I needed to keep 5 times as much opportunity in my pipeline as was required as baseline. That's $13,5000,000 * 5 = $67,500,000. I didn't achieve this on my own, of course, I had a sales team below me who each had their own part of this pipeline. I also had a huge marketing team behind me, who theoretically were supposed to be helping fill the pipeline.

These types of quotas and calculations are what you will need to keep in mind when you are setting up your pipeline in Hubspot. The system keeps a running total of your total pipeline opportunity for you to keep an eye on.

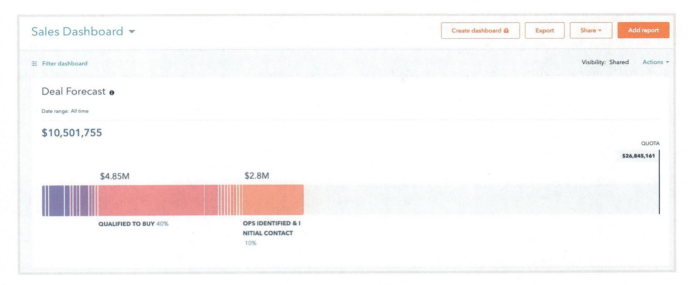

Weighted Average Sales Pipeline

This is a screenshot from my own pipeline filtered down to one subset of what we sell. Your's will look different and have different deal stages. If you know what your average deal size is, and you know what the sales quota is for an individual sales person or even for your company, you can then put marketing on a revenue target budget. When you get to this level of operational excellence, you will have turbocharged your marketing and sales machine.

What Should I Do To Start With

If you're a new company, you won't have much sales history to work with. However, if you're an existing company, I recommend you input at least the last 3 years of deals. This should provide you with plenty of information to determine what your average deal size, how long your sales cycle is and what's in your current sales pipeline. This, of course, depends on your average sales cycle. If it is very short, say 30 days, if your deal volume is very high, perhaps 90 days is enough. If, in the much more likely case that it is close to 6 months, or even 18 months, then more will be needed. But a little information can go a long way toward reducing uncertainty.[109]

Basic Setup Time

If you're an e-commerce company who is going to be using Hubspot with Shopify, during the trial, we'll be connecting up your system using the native integration. The value in this is that it will show you abandoned shopping carts and their value, even when you don't have contact information.

Using Inbound Marketing to Juice E-Commerce Sales

We often times implement an Inbound Marketing strategy with an E-Commerce store, usually on Shopify. During the trial, we won't be able to do the complete implementation, but what can be done is to use the Shopify Buy Button embedded on a Hubspot Landing page. This then provides you with the latest SEO ability of Hubspot, while providing an e-commerce capability. It doesn't matter whether you're selling a physical or digital product either. You can use this setup. Once live, we've gotten some incredible conversion rates using custom e-commerce enabled Hubspot templates. As Shopify also advises you that content is what you're going to need to produce to boost sales, in particular blogs and other related content offers, Hubspot

---

[109.]   Setting sales quotas is a tough challenge. There seems to be some mystery as to how to do it.

is the way to go here. Its blogging platform provides much better performance than Shopify's limited blog[110]. For e-commerce that still requires some human intervention, the predictive lead scoring can be particularly powerful in helping focus the sales effort.

Amazon Requires Time to Setup

It may be the elephant in the room when it comes to e-commerce, but it still requires considerable time and effort to set up and make work. A very common scenario we run across is Hubspot+Shopify+Amazon and many other Sales Channels. This is a case where traffic created by Hubspot and your content drives traffic to your Shopify Store, yet the sale is done on Amazon. Why? Because a huge percentage of the population are members of Amazon Prime. Aside from the fact that Amazon Prime has a conversion rate as high as 60%, many stores provide the ability to pay with Amazon Payments, on the store. For the consumer that has an Amazon Prime account, with all their payment details there, this is just an easier way to shop.

But Can I track It?

Short answer, yes you can. Hubspot will cookie a visitor, and you can also do a lot with tracking URL[111]'s and UTM[112] codes. If a customer then buys something, in many cases, you can see when they first hit your site,

---

[110.] For Hubspot Enterprise users, you can detect events. These events can be used to trigger e-mails and phone calls as well. They can also be combined with Predictive Lead Scoring for even better results.
[111.] URL - Uniform Resource Locator which is a web page location
[112.] UTM - Urchin Tracking Module, a type of tracking code you can add in to URLs which provide additional information for analytic purposes.

then ultimately, how long it took them to become a customer and what they bought from you. Now you have information you can use to create a lookalike audience on Facebook, from which you can drive traffic to Amazon. It's not perfect analytics, but it's still very powerful.

Google

What the Heck is PPC?

PPC stands for Pay-Per-Click. Though that's easy enough to understand, how they actually charge an advertiser can take many forms. It can be when someone clicks. Or it can be when someone watches a certain amount of a video on YouTube. Or, and here is where it gets interesting, it can be when someone buys something. How you pay is determined upon your bid strategy, while the cost is based on a whole raft of other factors. One of the more powerful bid strategies is Target Return on Ad-Spend or TROAS. Here's how that works. Let's say you would be happy to spend a dollar to make five. In other words, you're looking to make a 500% return on your ad-spend investment. You set this up in your Google Ads settings, and Google goes to work. You will see a sudden spike in traffic, and then if you have a high converting offer, Google will send enough traffic to your site to achieve your TROAS[113].

There are many other types of bid strategies, both manual and automated. I am not going to give you a recommendation for any particular one, as it is likely they have changed their offering by the time you read this. Of course, the answer depends on your goal, but that's not always easy to set, see Chapter One, Growth and Revenue. What's much more important to understand is that Google grades your funnel, page-by-page,

---

[113.]   This is one of several bidding strategies you may use.

and won't send traffic your way if it gives you a poor grade. They won't take your money if they don't think they can make the sale.

How Many Types of Google Ads Should I Use?

Unfortunately, I have to give you the standard consultant answer, "it depends." There are a variety of ad types and ad networks you can target. I personally do most of my PPC work using simple word ads. For e-commerce, I use Google PLA (Product Listing Ads), which flow via the Google Merchant Center. Google is increasingly driven by Artificial Intelligence, which means many of the different ads are constantly changing, as should your strategy.

Ninja Level Tricks

When you're learning Google Adwords, you'll struggle to come up with effective ads. One of the more useful features of the tool is its ability to 'spy' on what competitors are doing. In essence, it will show the ads of what Google considers a competitor of yours. You then can see what your competitors think is important for their customers to know about them. You can't just copy your competitor ads, but you do have inspiration.

You can also find out some key information here that affects how much you will pay, namely, your Google Quality Score, which is a grade they give to whichever page you're sending traffic to. If your quality score is low, your cost will be higher and your conversion rate will most likely be lower than it otherwise would be.

You can also use the tool to target users when they're most likely to be searching. If your business uses a call center, you'll want to use the information to adjust your call center staffing hours.

You can also use various sources of information to create audiences within the tool. For instance, let's say you have a YouTube channel; you can create an audience not just of viewers, but of subscribers, those who viewed a certain percentage of a video, or those that clicked on a link.

There's a lot more you should know about running PPC on Google, of course, and it takes a while to get it dialed in. Once you do, it can have incredible results.

How Much Does Google PPC Management Cost?

Though there is no hard and fast rule as to what you should expect to pay an Agency to manage your Google Ad-Spend; it is easy enough to find some price points on the internet. I usually charge a client using one of two models:

◆ A percent of Ad-Spend (plus set up fees)
◆ A percent of Sales
◆ A combination of both

For a percent of Ad-Spend model, you can expect to pay about 12% to 15% a month for ad-spend up to $15,000 a month, and for enterprise level ad-spend, for monthly ad-spend of $1 million to $1.5 million, you can expect to pay about $50,000 a month or 10%, whichever is greater. For monthly ad-spend above

$2 million, you can expect to pay about $85,000 a month or 15%, whichever is greater. Many clients also do a percent of sales combination model, but this requires complete transparency to all backend systems. Unless a client is on a system such as Hubspot or Salesforce, this becomes infeasible. But I have and do run major, multi-million dollar Google PPC campaigns with this type of model. The advantage to a client to a percent of sales model is that usually you do not pay for the 2nd and subsequent sales derived from a PPC driven conversion.

When it comes to e-commerce stores, it easier to mix and match the models because you can see the revenue being generated. Many, if not most, start-up e-commerce stores do their own PPC, then eventually bring on an agency as they realize it is not their forte nor a good use of their time. One model I've consistently been able to work is helping start up a new e-commerce store from zero, since there's a lot of moving parts, including ad-spend, to get set up.

Look What I Found Out

The Google Search Console[114], which you can access both directly and from within Google Analytics, provides information on both technical and functional aspects of your website. One of the most important pieces of information it provides are the search terms people are using when they found your page. It can also reveal a lot about the performance of particular landing pages on your website, all from within the Google Analytics interface.

---

114. Referenced 2019: https://search.google.com/search-console/about

One of the key uses for the Search Console is to determine what the average position is of your page for a particular search term. If you're targeting a branded keyword but your position is much below 3, you're not getting clicks for it.

What Were They Using When They Found Me

You may not realize this, but much of your traffic is from mobile devices these days. What you really need to know, though, is whether mobile traffic converts or whether they start their search on mobile and ultimately convert on their desktop. Google Search Console is the tool where you start to figure this out. If knowing what type of device they were on is important, then knowing where they were at is also important. No need to target users in Japan if you only sell in the USA.

The Magic of Google Search Console and Hubspot Integration

One of the recent integrations released by Hubspot is integration[115] to the Google Search Console. With it, you can see what terms people were using in Google when Google decided to show a particular page. You can also see the number of impressions your particular page received for a particular keyword and as well, how many clicks your page received from these impressions. So what, you say.

Here's why this bit of integration magic is a big deal. You see, up until about 2012-2014, within Hubspot, you could see which keywords people were using when they found your page. Then google began to encrypt

---

[115].   Referenced 2019: https://app.Hubspot.com/ecosystem/118735/marketplace/apps/marketing/seo/google-search-console

virtually all search traffic in the name of privacy. Prior to this event, you did your keyword research within Hubspot, which allowed you to create a list of target keywords. Then you built your content offer around a keyword, in particular, a long tail keyword. You were looking for a particular set of characteristics when you built this list. You were looking for a search volume of at least 100 per month and a difficulty level of 50 or below.

Then, Google changed the world, mostly so you would have to buy ads, not get clicks from organic. There were many other changes made by Google at the same time, and many more are being made everyday (about 3,500 a year just to the search algorithm). Google Analytics can tell you a lot but you need to be a Google Analytics guru to know how a particular page performed. Plus you need to be in Google to use it. With this integration, you're now back inside your Hubspot system, working at the page level, which is where you want to be. This is a huge advantage to have from a systems standpoint.

What Can You Do With All This Data?

A/B test of course! When you take a look at the optimization tab of any specific Hubspot page, and it has dozens or hundreds of entries in it, you have data with which to start creating a never ending stream of A/B test using that data. Beyond A/B tests, though, you can simply use the data provided by the Hubspot optimizer to improve the existing page. I do this constantly, and have seen a steady improvement in my conversion rates. It also means you can and should create Google PPC ads for your pages that incorporate this new search data. You will see an improved quality score and lower ad cost and better conversion rate data. I've included a shot of what you will see inside Hubspot (keep in mind, these are always as of the time of publication and most likely will have changed by the time you see this in your own system)

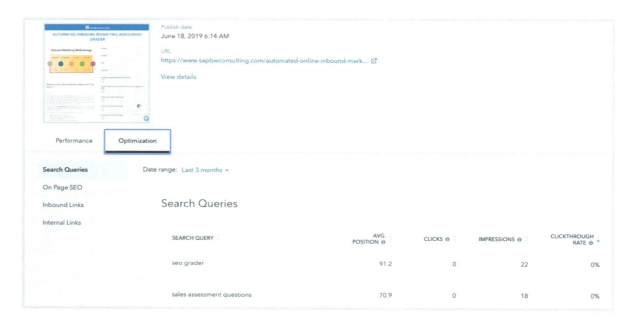

Drilling Down In To The List of Search Queries

Search Queries

SEARCH QUERY	AVG. POSITION	CLICKS	IMPRESSIONS	CLICKTHROUGH RATE
keyword grader	30.1	0	1,734	0%
preparing for an inbound marketing assessment	22	0	72	0%
marketing grader	82.3	0	39	0%
seo grader	91.2	0	22	0%
online sales assessment	74	0	20	0%
sales assessment questions	70.9	0	18	0%
inbound marketing assessment	22.7	0	9	0%

The list of search queries shown above is about one-fourth of the search queries actually shown in the list. It is to give you an idea of the information available. In this case, I've also sorted the page on impressions[116]. I can see people are being shown this page when they search for keyword grader, yet I am not receiving clicks. That is because this page is not a keyword grader. Now I have actionable insight with which I can make improvements to the page, now and in the future.

Free But Powerful

Google Analytics[117] is a free analytical tool provided by Google. You should know they also offer a much more powerful paid version, but for the majority of smaller enterprises, GA will be what they use. To install it, you create a Google Property, grab the tracking code, and install it, following the directions provided by Google and whatever platform you're installing it on. You should also realize that though the Universal Analytics code is supposed to be 'Universal', you will, in fact, have to add various pieces of code to it as you increase the complexity of your GA setup. For instance, if you create Custom Dimensions, these have a code that has to be added.

Basic Setup Tasks For Success

After your Universal Analytics Tracking Code is installed, I usually set up my Goals, which you do in the admin section of the tool. I recommend at least the following three goals:

[116.] Impressions, in this case, means how many people saw this in their search results. There are additional elements to be aware of when talking about impressions.

[117.] Referenced 2010-2019: https://analytics.google.com/

1. Smart List
2. Shopping Cart Add
3. Checkout Complete.

If you don't have a shopping cart, then the Thank You page of whatever you consider to be the final step in someone converting on your website before being contacted by sales. These goals will need to be imported into Google Adwords in order for it to optimize properly.

It's usually convenient to map and set up your SalesFunnel while you're doing this. This means you will need to start at the top of your website and enter the information a user would enter and keep going all the way through to the "Thank You" page of your funnel. The system will then start to measure the visitors to each stage of your funnel and as well, the conversion rate from one stage of your funnel to the next.

You will also need to set up your Google Search Console[118], which also involves a process for verifying your ownership of your website. There are various settings you need to make in order for Google to collect information. In general, the answer is yes, but not always.

You will also need to connect your social media accounts or at least the social media plug-ins that allow you to do this.

You can also input cost information here, and if you know your cost, I recommend you do. Then you can have a much clearer idea of what your true ROI is from your Ad-Spend

---

[118.] Referenced 2010-2019: https://search.google.com/search-console/about

Once You're Up and Running

Once you're all set up, you will start to see information coming in about your website traffic - including whether you have any or not. Now you can monitor Real Time traffic, goal conversion rates and campaign results. The challenge is to figure out the minimum amount of information you need to monitor, otherwise, the rabbit hole is very deep here.

The E-Commerce Side of Google Ads

The Google Merchant Center[119] is a separate Google property which is used to enable you to run Product Listing Ads (PLA). What's a PLA? If you go to Google Search and do a search for a product, such as Red High Heels, you will see a series of boxes with Red High Heels and links to the shopping carts of the various vendors. If someone clicks on these ads, they will be taken straight to that vendors shopping cart for that product. In short, they have just demonstrated a high degree of buying intent.

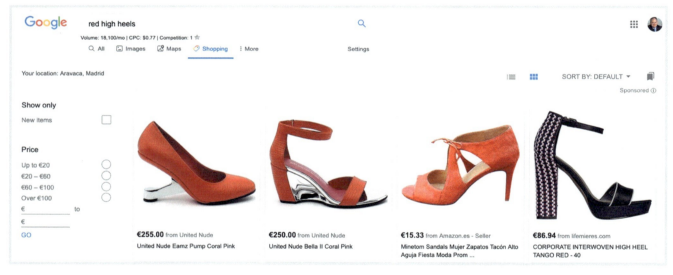

Google and the Google logo are registered trademarks of Google LLC, used with permission.

However, you don't actually run the ads on Google Merchant Center, you run them in Google Adwords[120] as Google Shopping Campaigns. In order to do all this, you first have to get the product information from your store to the Google Merchant Center. To do this, you have to provide a data feed, which can be a CSV spreadsheet,

---

119.   Referenced 2010-2019: https://www.google.com/retail/solutions/merchant-center/
120.   Referenced 2014-2019: https://ads.google.com/intl/en_ES/home/

or via a Product Data Feed provider, such as ShoppingFeeder. I highly recommend you use a data feed provider unless you just have a small number of products which never change and for which you will never change the prices or run a sale or offer free shipping or other incentives. The secret sauce of successful PLA ads is the data feed.

The upside of running PLA ads is that they pull all their information from what you have in your product descriptions. That means you must have high quality product images, SEO optimized listings, and the right offer. This is also the downside of the system. You don't really have much control over what Google does with it, and in my experience, most owners will routinely find things they don't like about some aspect of what Google is presenting and ask the agency to fix it. Unfortunately, this is a Sisyphean task[121]. As you will learn, all improvement should be taking place in the product listing page.

One Tag Manager to Rule Them All

The Google Tag Manager, yet another Google tool, is designed to allow you to put one tracking code on your website, and then add tags from other platforms, such as Facebook and Twitter and a huge list of others. It has continuously evolved over time and today, is a generally useful tool. Unfortunately, it is rarely the case where you don't have to add additional tracking code here and there. I do recommend you use it, but to be aware that it is not for the casual user.

That said, I've implemented it on a large number of properties with a successful outcome. It's really the only tool that allows you to see all the tags you have installed on your site (at least it's the only free tool), and to see how they are working. If you need to make a change to a trigger, this is the quickest way to do it.

---

121.   Viewed: https://www.youtube.com/watch?v=kkgTWRakUN8

Don't Reinvent The Wheel

For the normal user, who wants to focus on building the business, and not so much on working for Google, which is what you will feel like most days, I recommend you hire a Google Tag Manager specialist[122] to install and set up your GTM. It's a lot easier to add tags once the installation is done correctly. For many setups, such as Shopify, there are plug-ins that are really preconfigured GTM properties. For instance, for about 99 dollars, you can get a very comprehensive GTM setup from a company called Elevar[123]. There's a small but growing army of GTM experts out there. They exist because setting up Google Analytics and all of the other Google properties is not as simple as it should be. In fact, most marketers find they are nearly constantly tweaking some setting within the Google setup. Don't expect that change.

The Elephant Herd in the Room

You may already have an idea of some of the numbers: More than 2 Billion users globally. People spend many waking hours on the platform. What you may not realize is how many different properties Facebook owns. For example, messenger, the most used messaging app in the world. Or Instagram, bought by Facebook and now where all the cool people hang out. It owns properties in China, is constantly buying more properties and has a very advanced advertising platform.

---

122. Referenced 2019: https://www.analyticsmania.com/
123. Referenced Nov, 2019, https://www.getelevar.com/

Yes, You Can Sell on Facebook

Facebook is primarily seen as a B2C platform, though I've seen some great results for B2B. Like Google Product Listing Ads, you can advertise your products directly from your store on Facebook. Unlike Google PLA ads, you can actually buy stuff on Facebook's e-commerce platform. You'll need a product data feed here, and you can use either a CSV file or a product data feed provider, like ShoppingFeeder. I highly recommend you use ShoppingFeeder[124].

The challenge with Facebook is learning and understanding the advertising platform, which serves both Facebook and Instagram. What you need to keep in mind is that Facebook is a social media platform, and that means you need to do more than just advertise. You need to be there, and be present, to be part of the community. I've now ran hundreds of thousands of dollars of highly profitable campaigns on Facebook for a wide cross-section of clients in various business categories. I believe it is and will continue to be, a very good channel to spend your advertising dollars on – if you can master it.

People Respond to Facebook Messenger Messages

Though I expect people to eventually stop responding to the noise on Facebook Messenger, for now, in 2020, you get extremely high response rates. What works exceptionally well is a well designed Chatbot monitored by a human. I've set up some really complex conversational bots using ManyChat[125]. It collects contacts on a regular basis, in the thousands, and makes sales. But that is a tool that resides inside messenger. It is also an excellent customer relationship management tool, for example, for providing shipment notifications, running

---

124. Referenced 2014-2019: https://www.shoppingfeeder.com/
125. Referenced 2014-219: https://manychat.com

calculations or providing order confirmations. WeChat in China is a primary e-commerce channel for many, many businesses and I expect Facebook Messenger will be as well once the testing phase is completed.

Your Facebook Content Plan

Success on Facebook comes down to both having a budget that makes sense and having content specific to Facebook. Facebook loves video, of course, but you're going to need long form content as well as still pictures, and fans, lots and lots of fans. The winning strategy here is to combine TOFU, MOFU, BOFU thinking and content with ads that support each type. But you should lean heavily on the conversion type ad.

Instagram should be treated as a separate platform with its own rules, of course. You still manage the ads from the Facebook ads platform. It is a highly visual social media platform, which means pictures and lately, video. If your product makes people look good or feel good, this is your go to channel. At least that has been my experience.

Facebook groups are also a very important marketing tool for the average business. What are Facebook Groups? Just what they sound like, a way to gather people with a common interest into one spot on Facebook, called a group. When managed correctly, you can create a group of highly engaged people around your brand. What seems to work best, at least from a marketing standpoint, is educational groups. Not all businesses will fit this particular model, but for many, it should be a major investment area.

Our Call To Action

We offer the full suite of Inbound Marketing and Inbound Sales services. You can <u>book us now</u> for an entire project or on an hourly basis. However, spaces are limited. Or, you can get a free one hour consultation by booking some time on my <u>calendar</u>.

Why Should You Hire Us?

Simply put, I know from experience that it takes far more than just Inbound Marketing to dominate a market. That's why I wrote this book. I've never had a customer who needed only Inbound Marketing. They've needed skills that come from knowing about each element of business, from sales, marketing, finance, logistics, IT, Human Resources and Organizational Change, as well as the extended Supply Chain. Sounds a lot like what large scale ERP projects require. But we've helped enough start-ups get to IPO or acquisition to realize that many need less to do more. Only intelligently applied advanced technology and methodology can make that happen.

Make the Call.

CHAPTER SIX

SUMMARY

Summary

You now have the knowledge to build a turbocharged digital sales and marketing system. If it is not apparent, there's a lot more to it than you may have thought. It is an ever changing environment, with thousands of new marketing and sales applications brought to market in just the past 10 years.

You cannot and should not attempt to master them all. Instead, build a solid business foundation, know what you sell, then use this book as your master design guide. You will keep hearing new terms, like digital transformation, the New Sales, Inbound Marketing, Artificial Intelligence, Machine Learning, IoT and many others.

You will need to focus on building out your system of systems. In fact, focusing is the challenge. It is a constant challenge to avoid getting distracted by the next shiny object. But, you will need to keep an eye out for the systems and strategies that are emerging as winners and which might help you. It has never been easier or cheaper to start a new business.But it has also never been as complicated.

Go forth and prosper.

CHAPTER SEVEN

ABOUT THE AUTHOR

Lonnie Ayers is a serial entrepreneur with a Fortune 500 background. He has over four decades of experience. With an MBA, BS, AAS and long distinguished career in the United States Air Force, he has taken several businesses from zero to one million and well beyond in revenue in under a year. He holds a PMP, is a Certified Scrum Master and SAFe certified, and holds or has held all available Hubspot Marketing and Sales Certifications. In addition, he is an SAP Certified Materials Management Consultant, SAP Certified Project Manager, SAP Strategic Enterprise Management and Kaplan-Norton Balanced Scorecard Certified Consultant.

He runs SAP BW Consulting, Inc. which is focused on helping companies develop high performance marketing and sales machines. He also still provides SAP Project Management consulting services, and strategic advisory services to a variety of clients, both large and small.

INDEX

BIBLIOGRAPHY

Benioff, Marc. 1999. *Salesforce.* Sept-Nov 1. Accessed Jan 7, 2020. https://www.salesforce.com/.

Brian Halligan, Dharmesh Shah. 2006. *Hubspot.* June 1. Accessed February 15, 2020. https://www.hubspot.com/.

Dixon, Matthew, and Brent Adamson. 2011. *The Challenger Sale.* New York, New York: Penguin Group.

Drucker, Peter. 1954. *The Practice of Management.* New York, New York: HarperBusiness.

n.d. *Five9 Cloud Contact Center Software.* Accessed March 11th, 2020. https://www.five9.com.

Goldratt, Eliyahu M. 1984. *The Goal A Process of Ongoing Improvement.* Vol. 2. Great Barrington, Massachusetts: North River Press.

Gravagna, PHD, Nicole, and Peter K Adams, MBA. 2013. *Venture Capital for Dummies.* Hoboken, New Jersey: John Wiley & Sons.

Halligan, Brian. 2016. *INBOUND 2016: Brian Halligan & Dharmesh Shah Keynote.* Hubspot. November 9th. Accessed August 4, 2016. https://www.youtube.com/watch?v=dnfwckhZiLc&t=18s.

Halvorson, Kristina, and Melissa Rach. 2012. *Content Strategy For The Web.* Berkeley, California: Pearson Education.

Hannan, Mack. 2004. *Consultative Selling, The Hanan Formula for High-Margin Sales at High Levels.* Vol. Seventh Edition. New York, New York: American Management Association.

Hill, Napoleon. 1937. *Think and Grow Rich.* New York, New York: Fawcett Books.

Hubbard, Douglas W. 2009. *The Failure of Risk Management.* Hoboken, New Jersey: John Wiley & Sons.

2011. *Hubspot Academy.* Hubspot. Mar 1. Accessed Mar 11, 2020. https://academy.hubspot.com/.

Kaplan, Robert S, and David P. Norton. 2008. *The Execution Premium.* Boston, Massachusettes: Harvard Business Press.

Koch, Richard. 1997. *The 80/20 Principle, The Secret of Achieving More With Less.* London: John Murray Press.

Kurlan, Dave. 2006. *Baseline Selling.* Bloomington, Indiana: authorhouse.

2003. *LinkedIN.com.* Sept 1. Accessed Aug 1-5, 2017. https://www.linkedin.com/learning/lead-generation-foundations-2015/define-your-target.

Marshall, Perry. 2013. *80/20 Sales and Marketing: The Definitive Guide to Working Less and Making More.* Irvine, California: Entrepreneur Press.

—. 2017. *Ultimate Guide to Facebook Advertising: How to Access 1 Billion Potential Customers in 10 Minutes (Ultimate Series), 3rd Edition.* Irvine, California: Entrepreneur Press.

—. 2017. *Ultimate Guide to Google AdWords: How to Access 100 Million People in 10 Minutes (Ultimate Series), 5th Edition.* Irvine, California: Entrepreneur Press.

McAfee, Andrew. 2019. *More from Less: The Surprising Story of How We Learned to Prosper Using Fewer Resources—and What Happens Next.* New York, New York: Scribner.

McCoy, Julia. 2020. *A Case Study in Blogging: 21,600 Keyword Rankings in Google and 90,000 Visitors Per Month .* March 9th. Accessed March 9, 2020. https://expresswriters.com/blogging-case-study/.

—. 2019. *The Expert SEO Content Writer.* Julia McCoy. August 1. Accessed March 17, 2020. https://students.seowritingcourse.com.

Michalko, Michael. 2001. *Cracking Creativity.* Berkely, California: Ten Speed Press.

Mikita Mikado, Sergey Barysiuk. 2011. *Pandadoc.* Accessed December 17, 2019. https://www.pandadoc.com/.

Myler, Larry. 2010. *Indispensable by Monday.* Hoboken, New Jersey: John Wiley & Sons, Inc.

Reinertsen, Donald. 2009. *The Principles of Product Development Flow: Second Generation Lean Product Development.* Vol. 1 edition (2009). Redondo Beach, California: Celeritas Publishing.

Roberge, Mark. 2015. *The Sales Acceleration Formula: Using Data, Technology, and Inbound Selling to go from $0 to $100 Million.* Hoboken, New Jersey: Wiley.

Roetzer, Paul. 2014. *The Marketing Performance Blueprint.* Hoboken, New Jersey: Wiley.

Sheridan, Marcus. 2019. *They Ask, You Answer: A Revolutionary Approach to Inbound Sales, Content Marketing, and Today's Digital Consumer, Revised & Updated 2nd Edition.* Hoboken, New Jersey: Wiley.

Sutton, Robert I. 2007. *The No Asshole Rule, Building a Civilized Workplace and Surviving One That Isn't.* New York, New York: Grand Central Publishing.

Tyler, Marylou, and Jeremy Donovan. 2016. *Predictable Prospecting.* New York, New York: McGraw Hill Education.

Weiss, Alan. 2011. *Million Dollar Consulting Proposals: How to Write a Proposal That's Accepted Every Time.* Hoboken, New Jersey: John Wiley & Sons.

—. 2016. *Million Dollar Consulting: The Professional's Guide to Growing a Practice, Fifth Edition.* New York, New York: McGraw-Hill Education.

Printed in the United States
By Bookmasters